The Swing Era
Into the
'50s

EDITOR: George G. Daniels

Staff for THE SWING ERA: Into the '50s EDITOR: Philip W. Payne ADMINISTRATIVE EDITOR: Jeanne LeMonnier ART DIRECTOR: John R. Martinez STAFF WRITERS: David Johnson, Joan S. Reiter, Michèle Wood RESEARCHERS: Betty Ajemian, Lea Guyer, Suad A. McCoy, Florence McNeil, Joan Nierenberg, Karl F. Reuling, Barbara Richey, Eleanor Schwartz COPYREADER: Rachel Tuckerman CONSULTANTS: Dan Sibley (graphics), Joesph Kastner, Burt Korall, George T. Simon (editorial)

MANAGING DIRECTOR: Francis M. Scott III

GENERAL MANAGER: Peter L. Hoyt SALES MANAGER: Edmund Schooler
PROMOTION MANAGER: William C. Kiefer BUSINESS MANAGER: Terrance M. Fiore
PRODUCTION MANAGER: Roger C. Herrmann INTERNATIONAL OPERATIONS MANAGER: Charles C. Colt, Jr.
EUROPEAN MANAGER: Robert H. Smith ASIA MANAGER: Beto Yamanouchi

THE SWING ERA is produced in the United States by TIME-LIFE RECORDS in cooperation with CAPITOL RECORDS, INC. David D. Cavanaugh, Executive Producer, Bill Miller, Associate Producer, Editions outside the United States and Canada are produced in cooperation with Electric & Musical Industries, Limited, London, England, or its affiliated companies.

ON THE COVER: Professional Dancer Stanley Carron "shines", as he interpolates a kick into one of the Lindy Hop's basic steps, the Jig-Walk, which he demonstrates here with his partner, Kaye Popp. Gjon Mili took this photograph for LIFE in 1943.

The Swing Era
Into the '50s

How Sex Was Invented

The Men Who Made the Music:
Gene Krupa   John Kirby

The Music in This Volume

Discography

TIME-LIFE RECORDS

NEW YORK

How Sex Was Invented

Sex was invented on April 14, 1930, after school, on the southwest corner of Lafayette and Washington Avenues in Brooklyn, N. Y., by a girl named Ethel Dowd. Ethel and I were in fourth grade at the time and on our way home from classes at Adelphi Academy. When we got to that corner she reached out her Palmolived hand, brushed her fingers across my forehead and gently rumpled my hair. That was it. I walked down Lafayette in a daze while Ethel walked down Washington in a slink.

I knew that sex was too important to be talked about and I swore to keep the invention secret. I kept my part of the bargain but I think Ethel must have talked, because a great many people seem to have got word of it, including several who do not even speak English. I had never noticed any evidences of awareness of sex before April 14, 1930, but after that I suddenly started to see them everywhere. Movie actors seemed to be thinking about sex all the time. People in the papers and magazines, in books and on the radio began to be obsessed with it. Even the girl in the White Rock advertisement, who had never appeared to have a thought in her head, all of a sudden—and without changing her expression the least bit—started thinking about sex. I don't know how I could tell this, but I could.

I lived through the Swing Era in a state of astonishment and awe, watching the news of Ethel's invention proliferate until it occupied the whole country. Here and there someone would try to hold back the tide and there would be a valiant struggle, but it was always foredoomed. In 1933 the Los Angeles *Times* refused to print the words "sow bellies," which refer to the part of the hog that is made into bacon. The *Times* used "sow bosoms." At about that time, Walt Disney, who had been portraying cows in his films with realistic udders, decided, in view of the temper of the times, to present his cows in panties. Those were stirring days. The Iowa Farmers Union met in Des Moines to discuss one of the most brilliant bureaucratic ideas that has ever been suggested by Washington: the hunger of people during the Depression might be relieved if little pigs and pregnant sows were slaugh-

tered to keep them off the market. The Farmers Union denounced the notion and in its resolution changed the phrase "pregnant sows" to the French "*enceinte* sows."

Although I could not speak French I knew what "pregnant" meant. It meant someone who didn't say much. I learned this from a sentence I read in *True Confessions* in a barbershop—"Raoul stared at me, and his silence was pregnant." It seemed unfair to kill a lot of sows just because they were quiet. I also knew what bosoms were.

My Aunt Gertrude had a bosom two feet wide and a foot thick, all in one solid piece, on which she used to hang sharp-pointed jewelry that cut my ears when she made a lunge to hug me. I think I had the impression that at night she took off this bosom, which must have been as heavy as an oak log, and that maybe she kept it on a pair of andirons beside her bed. My friend Ethel didn't have a bosom, which was

one of the things I liked about her. It is true that Ethel had two small, separate bumps on her chest, but I could not see how these could be connected with anything as awful as a bosom. However, I did notice that when girls got older, they *all* had these lumps, even larger ones, and that they probably had something to do with sex. I noticed this because of what I saw on a billboard outside a theater.

There was a theater in Brooklyn in those days that was run by a man who must not have been very smart. First, he misspelled its name, calling it the Gayety, and second, he did not show movies. I could not figure out how he expected anybody to go to a theater where they did not show movies.

One day when I was walking past the Gayety, I realized that the man was not only *not* trying to keep the news of Ethel's invention quiet; he was actually advertising it. He had a huge sign that said: "20 Sexy Girls 20." There were also some photographs of some ladies who, while they were wearing clothes, were not wearing many of them. Naturally I wanted to find out how much the man or his girls knew about sex and what they were telling people, so I went up to the box-office window and inquired about the price of admission. The man did not see me, although I was standing there in plain sight. He looked to the right and then to the left and then straight over my head, but he kept failing to see me, so again I asked him how much it cost to get into his theater, and finally he looked down and saw me.

"Get out of here, you dirty little kid!" he said.

Well, that is certainly no way to run a successful theater,

I thought, but the man refused to let me in and so I went away. I later discovered that he would not let any of my friends into his theater, either. However, one of my friends had an older brother who could get into the Gayety any time he wanted, and this older brother told my friend what happened in the Gayety. He said that there were ladies in there, some of them at least 30 years of age, who slowly took off their clothes while walking around the stage. Not all of their clothes—they kept on their shorts and another piece of underwear called a brassière. At the very height of the show they would also remove the brassière, but then something would go wrong with the electrical wiring in the theater and all the lights on the stage would go out.

Neither my friend nor I could see why his brother kept going back to the Gayety. In later years, however, after I had seen a few entertainers such as Sally Rand, Ann Corio, Georgia Sothern and Gypsy Rose Lee, I came to realize that the older brother had not been totally lunatic.

In addition to the owner of the Gayety there were others, several of them publishers, who deliberately tried to spread the news about sex. Of course, there was nothing about it in *Captain Marvel*. The Captain never thought about sex. He was so pure-minded that, when he wanted to say something really strong, he would not say "Holy Moses!" He said "Holy Moley!" (The humorist Ring Lardner was an even better bowdlerizer than Captain Marvel. Lardner once wrote "Golly is in His Heaven.")

But there were other magazines, notably *Esquire*, that often alluded to sex in one way or another. When the first issue of *Esquire* appeared in 1933, it contained a picture of a girl by artist George Petty that automatically made you think of sex. Every month after that, for years, Petty produced a new girl for *Esquire* and put goodness knows what ideas into millions of people's heads.

In 1939 the graduating class at Princeton University elected George Petty as its favorite artist. Rembrandt was second. About all that was obvious to me as a boy, however, was that there was a great difference between Aunt Gertrude's bosom and Ethel's bumps, and that this man Petty had hit upon a fine compromise.

Later, when I learned a little about art, I could see what Petty's technique was. He produced his superhuman figures by making their legs and torsos longer than normal and their heads a good deal smaller. Then, using the newest art instrument, an air brush, he skillfully sprayed thin films of paint on his work to give it a three-dimensional look. Men who were forced to live without female company in colleges, barracks, jails and lighthouses used to tack Petty's girls on their walls and talk about such fine points of art.

News of sex traveled so fast and so far in those early days that it invaded even the unlikeliest areas of life. For example, crime occupies quite a few people in this country, but before the discovery of sex, I had thought that criminals stole money just because they wanted it, or shot other people only because they were sore at them.

It is by no means that simple. Sex is often involved. As early as 1931 word of Ethel's invention had spread from Brooklyn all the way to Arizona, where the ouija-board murder took place. During the Swing Era, many of us tinkered with ouija boards. "Ouija" is a combination of the French and German words for "yes," and the board is about the size of a breakfast tray, printed with the letters of the alphabet, the numbers from one to ten, and the words "yes" or "no." With the board came a little three-legged table, called a planchette. All you had to do was place your fingertips lightly on this planchette and it would begin to move across the board, pausing at letters and spelling out messages. *You* move the planchette, but the theory is that a ghost or spirit guides your hand to certain letters or numbers.

In any case, it happened that in 1933 a lady named Dorothea Irene Turley was living on a ranch in Arizona with her elderly husband, who was a retired naval officer, and her 15-year-old daughter Mattie. Mrs. Turley, a restless beauty-contest winner, had befriended a handsome cowboy. As soon as I read that in the paper, I suspected there was going to be something about sex.

When Mrs. Turley was not talking to the cowboy, she frequently passed the time with a ouija board, which gave her some immoral messages, the burden of which was that someone ought to eliminate Mr. Turley. Daughter Mattie described the crucial session:

"Mother asked the ouija board to decide between Father and her cowboy friend. As usual, the board moved around at first without meaning, but suddenly it spelled out that I was to kill Father. It was terrible. I shook all over. Mother asked

the ouija board if the shooting would be successful and it said that it would.

"She asked if he would die outright and it said no. We asked what should be used in the shooting and it said a shotgun. We asked if we would have the ranch and it said yes. We asked about the law, but it said not to fear the law, that everything would turn out all right. We asked how much the insurance would be and it said five thousand dollars.

"I tried to kill Father the next day but I couldn't. I lost my nerve. A few days later, though, I followed him to the corral. I raised the gun and took careful aim between the shoulders, but then I lost my nerve again. But I thought of dear Mother and what all this would mean to her. I couldn't fail. My hand was trembling awfully but I raised the gun and fired."

Mr. Turley survived for a while and he was angry. He said the ouija board was a rotten thing, often making his wife and daughter do things they shouldn't, and that occasionally the board had even given *him* bad advice.

At the trial the verdict went against Mrs. Turley and her daughter, but it was reversed after they had served short terms respectively in prison and reform school, and they were set free. I like to think it was because Mattie was so thoughtful of her mother.

The Battle of West 90th Street

Another thoughtful girl of the time was Helen Walsh, who was 16 when they electrocuted her friend Two-Gun Crowley. Two-Gun, whose real first name was Francis, was one of the most wanted men in the country, having committed by 1931 at least one murder, seven armed holdups and several automobile thefts while he was still in his teens. Indeed he was only 19 when the police got him, but *he* had already heard about sex, too. I could tell because of the place Two-Gun and Helen parked their car. The newspapers said it was a "lovers' lane" in Merrick, Long Island, near New York City. A friendly local cop, thinking it was not a good idea for teen-agers to be out so late at night in a place like that, came up to the car to speak to them. Two-Gun shot him dead.

Two-Gun and Miss Walsh then drove to Manhattan and were joined by a friend, Rudolph ("Fats") Duringer. They retired to an apartment on the top floor of a five-story building at 303 West 90th Street, where the city police soon traced them. The cops sneaked up the stairs, but Two-Gun heard them coming and suddenly flung open the apartment door to greet them. He must have been quite a sight, and I remember wondering whether he should really have been called Two-Gun, Five-Gun or even Seven-Gun. Both his trouser legs were rolled up above the knee and a gun was strapped to each calf. He also had a holster on each hip, one under his shoulder and a gun in each hand. He fired a volley at the police, slammed the door and the siege began.

The papers called it the "Battle of West 90th Street." It was by far the most spectacular domestic engagement—as opposed to the overseas battles of World War II—of the Swing Era. Some 300 cops soon reached the scene, some of them carrying rifles, shotguns, tear-gas grenades and ma-

chine guns. While most of the police struggled to hold back a crowd of 15,000 spectators, the sharpshooters and the heavy-weapons men went after Crowley.

In the apartment, Two-Gun scurried from window to window, shooting at policemen on the street and on nearby rooftops. Two-Gun's friend Fats Duringer was not a great deal of help—old Fats tried to hide under a daybed. However, he couldn't get under it, not because he was so big, but because Helen Walsh was already there. The police fired more than seven hundred (700) bullets into and through the apartment, wounding Two-Gun four times. Fats and Helen were not hurt except for the tear gas, which finally caused Two-Gun to surrender.

While the 700 bullets were whistling past her ears and Fats was trying to poke her out from under the bed, Helen found time to worry about her fingernails and to write a letter. Although it gives one the impression that she, too, had heard about sex, it is otherwise the sort of innocent note one might expect from an American girl of sweet 16. It is addressed "To Whom It May Concern" and it goes:

"If I die and my face you are able to see, wave my hair, make me look pretty and make my face up. Dress me in black and white in a new dress. Do my nails all over, I don't use this kind of polish, it's too dark. I use a very pale pink. I always wanted everybody to be happy and have a good time —I had some pretty good times myself. Love to all but all of my love to Sweets. Helen Walsh"

"P. S. Everybody happy & how."

At the trial Miss Walsh testified against Two-Gun, or Sweets, and he was electrocuted. So was Fats Duringer, who admitted having committed a casual murder of his own somewhere. Miss Walsh was set free—the district attorney ap-

preciated her testimony and the jury was favorably impressed with her, perhaps because she was so tidy about her grooming.

Grooming, which included the care of one's teeth, gums and breath, was important to us in the Swing Era. We had a lengthy advertisement that dealt with it. The ad resembled an illustrated short story and the scene was a psychiatrist's office. A girl came in, sobbing, "I want gaiety, friends, love," and then the psychiatrist himself took over the narrative:

" 'And you shall have them,' I promised her.

"Into a psychiatrist's chambers streams an endless tide of life's misfits—the lonely . . . the bitter . . . the repressed . . . the misunderstood.

"And now before me stood another. I was certain, and later examination proved me right, that there was nothing organically wrong with her. Her face, her body bloomed with beauty and vitality. Yet emotionally she was at the breaking point.

"Gently, I probed for her history. She was 28, single, college-bred, lived in a good home with parents of some means, but was definitely the recluse type.

" 'Men friends?'

"Her lips quivered as she leaned close to me. The flood tide of her emotion burst through the gates of her control.

" 'You've hit on it, Doctor. I'm lonely—desperately lonely,' she sobbed. 'Every girl I know is married, but no man seems to want me. They come. They go. I cannot hold them. Even my women friends seem to avoid me. I go nowhere . . . see no one. And oh, Doctor, I want gaiety, friends, admiration, love . . . love . . . love!'

"She had risen, and her face was almost against mine. In that instant I knew that I had spotted the cause of her trouble. It was obvious."

At that, the psychiatrist took a couple of quick steps away from the girl, let out his breath and recommended Listerine. Soon she was engaged to "a well-to-do Easterner who simply adores her."

Only—Not Alone

Suddenly, as I read that advertisement, it seemed to me that there might be someone in the advertising industry who was using sex as a means to sell things. In order to pursue this hunch I opened a copy of *Silver Screen* at random, and there at the top of the page was a picture of a pretty girl in a bathtub, naked of course. Above her a headline said: "ANN TOOK A CHANCE ON A BATH ALONE."

I was startled. I *always* took my baths alone. Even if Ethel had asked me to take a bath with her, which she certainly wouldn't have, I would have been too embarrassed to do it. And yet, here was this pretty girl in the tub and in a picture beside her were two young men who, it appeared, might have been in there with her if she hadn't been taking a chance. I had not been reading many advertisements, but I read that one quickly. It turned out that the headline was a literary mistake on the part of the man who wrote the ad.

The ad should have said that Ann took a chance on only a bath, or a bath only, not on a bath alone. She should also

have used MUM; the bath *and* the MUM would have made her dainty and the two young men would have liked her, instead of despising her the way they despise girls who take chances on baths only. Still, whatever the literary quality of the ad, it was plain that its author had sex in the back of his mind. And the more I looked at other advertisements in other magazines, the more I realized that sex in one way or another was being used to sell laundry soap, automobiles and even Dynamic Tension.

Dynamic Tension was invented by Charles Atlas. An advertisement in *Dime Detective* in 1933, in comic-strip form, was called "The Insult That Made a Man Out of Mac," and it showed a very thin young man seated on a beach with a girl. Along came a big bully who deliberately kicked sand in Mac's eyes and said, "I'd smash your face—only you're so skinny you might dry up and blow away." Mac was at a loss for words, but soon he got up and went away and took the Charles Atlas Dynamic Tension Course. He came back bulging with muscles and found the bully, who was still sitting on the beach, beat him up and got the girl. It was a subtle treatment of the subject, but it was sex again.

Bowdlers at the Barricades

Although sex was seeping into advertising as well as into magazine art and the news, there were still men in journalism who struggled to defend the barricades. In 1934 a play called *Within the Gates,* by Sean O'Casey, opened on Broadway, and the audience was forced to read in the program that one of the characters was called "The Young Whore." Next day the New York *Times,* the *Post* and the *Telegraph* printed the word, but the *Sun* said "The Young Prostitute" while the *World-Telegram* used "The Young Harlot." The noble old

American, however, called her "A Young Girl Who Has Gone Astray."

There were also those in the radio industry who did their part to hold the line. In 1934 Dr. Thomas Parran Jr., who was soon to become Surgeon General of the United States Public Health Service and who fought a prolonged battle against venereal disease in this country, wanted to make a speech mentioning syphilis on the CBS network. When he submitted an advance copy to the CBS censors, however, they quickly put him in his place. It would be all right to talk about the awful consequences and symptoms, they said, but he would not be allowed to utter the word "syphilis" on the air. People would just have to guess what he was talking about. Dr. Parran angrily withdrew his speech and listeners were permitted to hear an interlude of recorded music.

Radio was not always so vigilant, however. In the mid-'30s there emerged a new phenomenon, the disc jockey, and soon most big cities had late-night stations that played romantic songs requested by listeners. Thus a disc jockey might mention a lady's name, her phone number or address, and then he would play her request, which was often *Empty Bed Blues, I Ain't Got Nobody* or *Lover, Come Back to Me.* When the import of that sank in, there would be races to see who would reach the lady first, the customers or the vice squad.

Still another force opposed to the burgeoning of sex was Tarzan, the Ape Man. Most of us were pretty sure he was fictional, but we forgot about that as soon as we got a few sentences into the latest account of him set down by Edgar Rice Burroughs. In the 1930s Tarzan had his only encounter with sex and it was exciting. Oh, it is true that he did a little hand-holding with Jane and the Countess Olga de Coude when Burroughs first discovered him, but for 20 years after that Tarzan wouldn't hold anyone's hand. He kept saying, "Women would contaminate us. We are not allowed to have them. If we were to succumb to their wiles, we would live in torment forever." But only a few years after Ethel's discovery, word of it reached Tarzan in Abyssinia. Burroughs reported what happened in *Tarzan and the City of Gold.*

Tarzan was taken prisoner by the armed forces of Cathne, the City of Gold, and as a result made the acquaintance of Nemone, Queen of Cathne.

"That she was marvellously beautiful by the standards of any land or any time grew more apparent to the lord of the jungle as she came nearer to him, yet her presence exhaled a subtle essence that left him wondering if her beauty were the reflection of a nature all good or all evil, for her mien and bearing suggested that there could be no compromise— Nemone, the Queen, was all one or all the other. She fascinated him; but whether as a thing of beauty or a thing of evil, he did not know. He only knew that few women, other than La, the High Priestess of the Flaming God, had ever so wholly aroused his interest and his curiosity. . . .

"A girdle about her hips was of gold mesh. It supported another ivory triangle the slender apex of which curved slightly inward between her legs and also her scant skirt of black monkey hair that fell barely to her knees, conforming perfectly to the contours of her body. . . . Her feet were shod with dainty sandals; and as she moved upon them silently across the stone floor, her movements seemed to Tarzan a combination of the seductive langour of the sensualist and the sinuous grace and savage alertness of the tigress. . . .

Nemone, Queen of Cathne

"Nemone's dark eyes, veiled behind long lashes, appraised the ape-man, lingering upon his bronzed skin and the rolling contours of his muscles; then rising to the handsome face until her eyes met his . . . . What strange eyes were hers—so beautiful, with fires burning far beneath the surface, so mysterious!"

The Queen summoned Tarzan to the palace and entertained him in a chamber decorated with gold, ivory and "the skin of a man tanned with the head on." Chained between two of the golden Doric columns was the Queen's pet lion, Belthar, who took an instant dislike to Tarzan. Not so the Queen. "Nemone extended a hand and laid it on his, a soft, warm hand that trembled just a little . . . . She fascinated him; she seemed to exercise a subtle influence, mysterious, hypnotic . . . .

"'I will make you a noble of Cathne,' whispered Nemone. She was sitting erect now, her face close to Tarzan's. He could feel the warmth of her body close to his; the aura of some exotic scent was in his nostrils; her fingers closed upon his arm with a fierceness that hurt."

Nemone started offering to make Tarzan rich, to load him down with golden helmets and with lions, which were the principal livestock of Cathne.

"The lord of the jungle felt weak beneath the spell of her burning eyes. 'I do not want *such* things,' he said. Her soft arm crept up about his neck. A tender light, that was new to them, welled in the eyes of Nemone, the Queen of Cathne. 'Tarzan!' she whispered."

Something came up to interrupt this conversation. "Tarzan shook himself as might a lion; he drew a palm across his eyes as one whose vision has been clouded by a mist; then he drew a deep sigh and moved toward the doorway . . . but whether it was a sigh of relief or regret, who may say?"

The next time they met, Nemone was at it again.

" 'Why are you not nice to me, Tarzan?'

" 'I wish to be nice to you, Nemone,' he replied, 'but not at the price of my self-respect . . . .' "

The Queen offered to build Tarzan a palace of his very own and actually got him to admit: " 'Were you a little more human, Nemone, you would be irresistible.' "

Nemone wasn't one of those girls who have to be coaxed. "She took him by the hand then and led him toward the door-

The man behind the cartoons

Whitney Darrow Jr., who drew the illustrations for this essay, including the self-portrait above, offers the following information about himself:

I was born on Aug. 22, 1909, in Princeton, N.J. My father was over 6 ft. tall, but I was only a foot and a half, weighed 7½ lbs. and had a red, wrinkled face. People said, "Isn't he funny-looking!" As I recall, people looked pretty funny to me, too. When I was six we moved to Upper Montclair and I fell madly in love with a girl named Ethel who rode a horse. From that day on I have been in love with horses.

I had just about developed immunity against New Jersey mosquitoes when in 1918 the family moved to Greenwich, Conn. I threw myself wholeheartedly into fifth-grade politics and the next February got two handsome valentines in addition to the five I had put into the school box for myself. In high school I wrote for the paper, acted in plays and played football—for two and a half minutes until a fullback ran around my end. At Princeton University, I found I still couldn't spell so I started filling my letters with pictures. This soon developed into my first cartoon for the Princeton Tiger.

I had majored in medieval history, so upon graduating in 1931 I naturally chose gag cartooning as a profession and sold cartoons first to Judge, *then to other magazines and eventually to* The New Yorker. *I wear rubber-soled shoes when at work because I feel it gives my cartoons a certain resiliency. I used to build things, like an indirect lighting system that left the room in total darkness; but I now have no hobbies unless you count golf, bowling and occasionally repairing the dam behind my house in Wilton, Conn., where I live with my wife Mildred. I have published four collections of my cartoons and have illustrated the works of several other authors, none of which gave me more pleasure than this delightful essay by Mr. Wallace.*

way of her chambers. 'In here, alone together, you shall teach Nemone how to be human.' "

Before the lesson could get under way they were interrupted *again* but fate kept bringing them together and the Queen never let up, even when Tarzan told her: "Do not be a fool, Nemone. I do not like fool women." By the next page she had worked Tarzan up to saying, "You are very beautiful, Nemone . . . ."

"She pressed against him, caressing his shoulder with a smooth, warm palm. 'Love me, Tarzan,' she whispered, her voice husky with emotion.

"There was a rattling of chains at the far end of the room, followed by a terrific roar as Belthar sprang to his feet. Nemone shrank suddenly away from the ape-man; a shudder ran through her body, and an expression, half fright, half anger, suffused her face. 'It is always something,' she said irritably . . . ."

The Queen took Tarzan off to the temple to listen to her pray to Thoos, the lion-god, for "the love of the one man in all the world that Nemone has ever loved! . . . and a great pity rose in the breast of the ape-man for this poor Queen who had never known love and who never might because of the warped brain that mistook passion for affection and lust for love."

All Power to the Flower

Probably out of pity, Tarzan dropped by the palace and got Nemone out of bed in the middle of the night. She entered, wearing "a light scarf," and lay down on a couch where she "sank among the soft cushions" and "motioned Tarzan to her side. . . . Her warm breath was on Tarzan's cheek as she drew him down beside her. . . . Her soft, bare arms slipped quickly about his neck and drew him close. 'Tarzan! My Tarzan!' she almost sobbed. . . . 'Tell me that you love me, Tarzan, and I shall be happy!'

" 'A flower does not bloom in the seed,' he replied; 'it grows gradually, and thus love grows. The other, that bursts forth spontaneously from its own heat, is not love; it is passion. I have not known you either long or well, Nemone; that is my answer.'

"She turned away and buried her face in her arms as she sank to the couch; he saw her shoulders shaken by sobs, and pity filled his heart."

A night or two later Tarzan turned up for dinner with the Queen who assured him "there will be none to disturb us tonight."

"Again her voice was soft, her manner gentle . . . . Every soft line and curving contour spoke of femininity and gentleness and love; and in those glorious eyes smouldered a dreamy light that exercised a strange hypnotic influence upon him . . . .

"She leaned closer to him. 'Touch me, Tarzan,' she whispered softly.

"Drawn by a power that is greater than the will of man he placed a hand upon hers. She breathed a deep sigh of contentment and leaned her cheek against his breast; her warm breath caressed his naked skin; the perfume of her

hair was in his nostrils. She spoke, but so low that he could not catch her words.

"'What did you say?' he asked.

"'Take me in your arms,' she breathed faintly.

"He passed a palm across his eyes as though to wipe away a mist, and in the moment of his hesitation she threw her arms about his neck and covered his face and lips with hot kisses.

"'Love me, Tarzan!' she cried passionately. 'Love me! Love me! Love me!'

"She slipped to the floor until she knelt at his feet .... The lord of the jungle looked down at her, at a queen grovelling at his feet ...."

Tarzan was very upset. In fact, "all that was fine in him revolted." He spurned her "with a half growl" and started for the door, but the Queen summoned her guards and sent him off to prison until she could arrange to have him ceremoniously killed by her pet lion, Belthar.

On the occasion of their last meeting, while waiting for the festivities to begin, Tarzan admitted that, with all her faults, "I am drawn to you." The jungle lord added: "You are attracted to me ... and I to you though I hold in contempt your principles, your ideals, and your methods. It is strange, isn't it?"

"The woman nodded. 'It is strange,' she mused. 'I never loved one as I loved you, and yet I am going to kill you ....'"

She then sicced her pet lion, Belthar, on Tarzan but his pet lion, Jad-bal-ja, turned up and killed the Queen's pet lion. The Queen then killed herself. Tarzan buried her and "beneath the soft radiance of an African moon he stood with bowed head beside the grave of a woman who had found happiness at last."

It was very exciting when the power that is greater than the will of man got hold of Tarzan. Millions of us were interested in how it would turn out. There were quite a few who hoped the Queen would get her way, even if she was dirty-minded and wore a scant skirt of monkey hair that fell barely to her knees. However, the Lord of the Jungle was just too strong, and we never found out exactly what Nemone had in mind.

Not all of the warriors against sex in the Swing Era were fictional, of course, nor were they all ineffectual old ladies and bowdlerizing preachers. The Hays Office struggled against sex with grim intent. During the first few years of the 1930s Hollywood produced several movies that were thought by a good many people to be dirty. One of them, *The Story of Temple Drake,* was based on William Faulkner's novel, *Sanctuary,* and it translated Faulkner's celebrated scene of unnatural, violent sex almost intact to the screen. Another film, *Convention City,* dealt with a handful of drunken, lecherous salesmen engaging in activities that are not, to this day, regarded as wholesome.

The Other Common Escape

By 1934 it had become apparent that something would have to be done to clean up Hollywood's films. The behavior of Hollywood's people, as well, had begun to seem a trifle undignified to some observers. The café-society hostess Elsa Maxwell, who had lately made an expedition there, reported that, "Sex was the other common escape [booze was first] from boredom in Hollywood. I had seen dissolute behavior among Europe's decadent aristocracy, but the movie colony's utter lack of inhibitions revolted me. Actors who were instantly recognizable on every street in America openly picked up waitresses and young girls. The women had no more discrimination than the men. They took lovers for diversion as casually as they played bridge or golf . . . and publicly paraded lovers like exhibits at a livestock show."

The movement for reform came not from the movie producers, but from various religious groups, chiefly the Legion of Decency. The Legion, organized by Roman Catholic bishops and armed with the threat of boycott of films by all Catholics (and many Protestants) in the country, threatened to stab Hollywood in the box office. Panicked, the producers suddenly remembered that they already *had* a mechanism for self-censorship—the Hays Office, which was supposed to keep movies clean by enforcing the Motion Picture Production Code. If a producer violated the Code, he was denied a seal of approval by the Hays Office—and lacking a seal, he could not show his picture in most of the theaters in the U.S. This arrangement, which had been technically in effect but generally ignored for several years, was dusted off with great fanfare to mollify the Legion of Decency, and from 1934 onward it was taken very seriously indeed. The Production Code of that time, written by a Catholic layman and a Jesuit priest, is worth looking at (*see box, page 16*).

During much of the Swing Era, the Production Code was enforced by an Irishman named Joe Breen, who had friendly relations with the Jesuits, who are the Marine Corps of the Roman Catholic Church. The Jesuits took a sober attitude toward sex. The Rev. Francis X. Talbot, editor of the Jesuit weekly, *America,* wrote that "American civilization and the Catholic Church are in open conflict on practically every phase of sex. The Catholic view holds sex and its manifestation as sacred; the American view regards it as somewhat more serious than a sneeze." Although he was not himself a churchman, Joe Breen was an exceedingly moral man and a tough cookie. He was a graduate of the U.S. Consular Service and had been a newspaper reporter in Chicago in the great days of Ben Hecht and Charles MacArthur. When he undertook the role of enforcer of the Code it was with these words:

"Very well, gentlemen, I accept the job. But on one condition. And the condition is that you understand that I come from a race of people who have a long history of committing suicide—on the other guy!"

Under Breen's influence, or iron hand, almost every reference to sex, however sanctified, was deleted from the movies. Even the word "Ladies" on what was obviously the door of a public facility became "Ladies Lounge."

Although William Faulkner kept on writing, en route to the Nobel Prize, Hollywood temporarily lost interest in him and filmed *A Girl of the Limberlost, Anne of Green Gables* and *Mrs. Wiggs of the Cabbage Patch.* A Mae West movie in progress, which had been advertised as *It Ain't No Sin,* was released under a new title: *Belle of the Nineties.*

There were precious few risqué moments during Breen's tenure. Jack Vizzard, who has written about Breen in a fine book called *See No Evil,* tells us how Breen exerted his authority one afternoon on the MGM lot. He had been asked to give his opinion on a costume for a dance number. Joe came bouncing onto the set and saw a girl standing there covered with balloons.

" 'Is this the costume?' he demanded incredulously.

" 'This is it.'

"He stalked over to the girl who was beginning to feel silly.

" 'Hold still, darlin',' he told her.

"He took the stub of a cigar out of his mouth and put it to the nearest balloon.

"POP!

"Then the next one.

"POP!

"Then right down the line.

"POP! POP! POP!

"He turned on his heel and strode out. That was the end of the discussion."

In 1934 in *It Happened One Night,* a title that Breen passed with some misgivings, Clark Gable was allowed to take off his shirt in the presence of Claudette Colbert. He was not wearing any undershirt. Audiences were spellbound at the revelation, and the men's underwear trade is said to have suffered a slump. In 1939 Breen permitted Gable to utter a four-letter word in the last scene of *Gone with the Wind.* The nation quivered in delicious shock when Gable looked at Vivien Leigh and said it: "Frankly, my dear, I don't give a damn."

Keeper of the Code

That was as far as Breen would go. After a few years of his administration, a producer accosted him and said sarcastically that perhaps Hollywood had better get out of the film business and start selling milk, because Breen had made the movies so bland that little else could be sold any more. Breen's answer, which might have seemed to some a trifle absentminded for a Keeper of the Code, was: "Maybe that would be a goddam good idea. If people like you would get out of the way and sell milk, maybe it would free the screen of a lot of its cathouse crap, and decent people could sit down and enjoy themselves in the theater without blushing." On another occasion when a director questioned his honesty, Breen is said to have fetched him a belt on the chops that knocked him over a couple of rows of projection-room seats.

Breen's words, "cathouse crap," both appear in Webster's *Unabridged,* which is thought to be the best dictionary we have. Webster's is more or less right about "cathouse" but somewhat off the mark in regard to "crap," which it defines as "buckwheat." Generally, "crap" means either junk or nonsense, especially offensive or pretentious nonsense, and is used in that sense in polite or at least enlightened society. In 1936 H. L. Mencken's great work, *The American Language,* burst upon the world in its major revised edition,

Joe Breen's Guide To Making Movies Without Sinful Sex

The Motion Picture Production Code which Joe Breen (pictured above pondering the famous Case of the Producer's Brothers-in-Law) enforced covered a multitude of sins, but the subject which seems, beyond all others, to have entranced its framers was sex. Section II of the Code contained the following admonitions:

II. SEX

The sanctity of the institution of marriage and the home shall be upheld. Pictures shall not infer that low forms of sex relationship are the accepted or common thing.

1. Adultery and Illicit Sex, sometimes necessary plot material, must not be explicitly treated or justified, or presented attractively.

2. Scenes of Passion
a. These should not be introduced except where they are definitely essential to the plot.
b. Excessive and lustful kissing, lustful embracing, suggestive postures and gestures are not to be shown.
c. In general, passion should be treated in such manner as not to stimulate the lower and baser emotions.

3. Seduction or Rape
a. These should never be more than suggested, and then only when essential for the plot. They must never be shown by explicit method.
b. They are never the proper subject for comedy.

4. Sex perversion or any inference of it is forbidden.

5. White slavery shall not be treated

6. Miscegenation (sex relationship between the white and black races) is forbidden.

7. Sex hygiene and venereal diseases are not proper subjects for theatrical motion pictures.

8. Scenes of actual child birth, in fact or in silhouette, are never to be presented.

9. Children's sex organs are never to be exposed.

Sex also crept into other sections of the Code:

Complete nudity is never permitted . . . . Undressing scenes should be avoided. . . .

Dances suggesting or representing sexual actions or indecent passions are forbidden.

The treatment of bedrooms must be governed by good taste and delicacy.

The following titles shall not be used: Titles which are salacious, indecent, obscene, profane or vulgar . . .

In its list of "repellent subjects" like hanging, branding, electrocution and surgical operations which the Code said "must be treated within the careful limits of good taste" was also included "the sale of women or a woman selling her virtue."

And in the section headed "Profanity" the Code not only forbade "pointed profanity and every other profane or vulgar expression" but specifically ruled out the following:

Alley cat (applied to a woman); bat (applied to a woman); broad (applied to a woman); Bronx cheer (the sound); chippie; cocotte; God; Lord; Jesus; Christ (unless used reverently); cripes; fanny; fairy (in a vulgar sense); finger (the); fire; cries of; Gawd; goose (in a vulgar sense); 'hold your hat' or 'hats'; hot (applied to a woman); 'in your hat'; Madam (relating to prostitution); nance; nerts; nuts (except when meaning crazy); pansy; razzberry (the sound); slut (applied to a woman); S.O.B.; son-of-a; tart; toilet gags; tom cat (applied to a man); traveling salesmen and farmer's daughter jokes; whore; damn; hell (excepting when the use of said last two words shall be essential and required for portrayal, in proper historical context, of any scene or dialogue based upon historical fact or folklore, or for the presentation in proper literary context of a Biblical, or other religious quotation, or a quotation from a literary work providing that no such use shall be permitted which is intrinsically objectionable or offends good taste).

and numbers of people pored through it in search of unusual words. The book mentions "crap," but in no obscene or scatological sense. Mencken's long, informative sentence, of the sort that brings tears of joy to the eyes of lexicographers, is:

"To the carnival man a stand outside a show is a *ballystand,* concessions are *joints* or *hooplas,* a seller of cheap novelties is a *gandy-dancer,* a hamburger stand is a *grab-joint,* a fortune-teller's tent is a *mit-joint,* a photograph gallery is a *mug-joint,* cheap prizes are *slum* or *crap,* a snake-eater or other such freak is a *geek,* a gambling concession is a *flat-joint* and the man operating it is a *thief.*"

Breen's one-time associate, Jack Vizzard, recalls another example of the Breen probity:

"One Christmas morning he woke up to find a shining black Cadillac, adorned with an enormous red ribbon, standing in his driveway. He studied it goggle-eyed for a moment. He put on a bathrobe, marched down to the driveway, inspected the card dangling from the ribbon, and went stomping back upstairs. He called the manager of the offending studio at his home and told him, at a pitch which made it almost unnecessary to use the phone, 'to get that GOD-DAMN THING out of here—TODAY!' "

Before taking leave of Mr. Breen, the great censor, it is worth recounting a tale related by Jack Vizzard that reveals another aspect of the man. Breen was of the opinion that excessive violence is not good in movies and hit upon a practical way of reducing it. He ordered his assistants, when reading scripts that had been submitted for approval, ar-

bitrarily to cut the number of killings in half. If a producer asked for six murders, he could have only three. In accordance with this principle one of Breen's aides reduced a producer's budget of shootings from 20 to 10—and denied the producer a seal when the finished film showed 13.

The producer and his lawyer came to Breen's office to plead for a seal. The lawyer argued in vain. Finally, as Vizzard recalls it, the producer insisted, over his lawyer's objections, on speaking for himself.

" 'Mr. Breen,' began the producer, 'I tell you the truth. I'm guilty as hell. Sure I shot thirteen. But I got an excuse.'

" 'Tell me.'

" 'You got a wife, Mr. Breen?'

" 'Joe smiled knowingly. 'And six children.'

" 'Good, then you understand. I got a wife too. You got relatives?' [Breen nodded.]

" 'Me too. All on my wife's side.'

" 'You have my sympathies.'

" 'Yeah. And mainly I got three lazy bums of brothers-in-law. My wife's brothers, you know?'

" 'Breen nodded again.

" 'They won't work. So what do I do? My wife keeps nagging me to give 'em a job. Me, I don't want'm on the payroll, but I gotta keep my wife quiet. So suddenly I got a great idea. I put them on the payroll, but I fool the hell out of my wife. I give 'em the parts of heavies, and I get 'em

killed at the end of reel three. Blam, blam, blam. Now I'm rid of them, my wife's satisfied, but I got thirteen killings. I don't want thirteen killings, Mr. Breen. I want ten. But whatta you gonna do?'

" 'Joe, by this time, was grinning good naturedly. He turned to his assistant, Charles Metzger. 'Better to be in trouble with us than with his wife, huh, Charles?'

" 'Oh, definitely,' Metzger agreed.

" 'Issue a Seal,' ordered Joe.

" 'And next time,' assured the producer heartily, waving his cigar levelly at Joe, 'I promise you. Ten killings—no more. I carry those bums to the end of the picture.' "

For some reason news of sex continued to spread in spite of the efforts of men such as Mr. Breen. During the war, by which I mean the one popularly called World War II, I discovered that the news had traveled as far as the western Mediterranean. In 1943 I found myself walking down a street in Naples, Italy, carrying a gun, or more accurately wearing one in a U.S. Navy holster on my belt. I was dressed in my sailor suit. A young Neapolitan lad came up to me and offered to introduce me to his sister. I was touched by this gesture of friendship from an ally, even if he was a recent ally, but I did not think the time was opportune. The suburbs were still full of Krauts.

The young Neapolitan lad would not take "no" for an answer, however, so I accompanied him on a walk through a picturesque part of the city, headed toward his sister's residence. When we got there I heard a female voice exclaim, *"Achtung! Amerikaner!"* which made me wonder what sort of people the lad's sister had been associating with. Nevertheless I forced myself to go into the house.

It was evident that the sister had not been expecting visitors because she was not wearing any clothes. I apologized for disturbing her and offered to come back on the following Tuesday, but she insisted that I stay. I scarcely knew what to say, so I tried to make the best conversation I could and blurted out the first thing that came into my head, which was, "Sex was invented on April 14, 1930, after school, on the southwest corner of Lafayette and Washington Avenues in Brooklyn, N.Y., by a girl named Ethel."

The Italian girl said that American sailors are notoriously untruthful, and that sex had actually been invented in 1931 in Düsseldorf by someone named Helga.

Of course I could not believe that, so I said, "I wish to be nice to you, but not at the price of my self-respect."

At that the Italian girl suddenly became very earnest and I could see that she was trying to tell me what, in her poor way, she believed to be the real truth. *"Mama mià!"* she said. "Everybody knows that sex was invented by my uncle Giuseppe."

Knoblocker's Delicious Pills

Her uncle Giuseppe? I thought. *Great Heavens!* How sad it is that humankind so often deceives itself, and what follies it pursues! I immediately took my leave of the girl and went back to my ship. The entertainment that evening during Happy Hour was a recorded lecture by Dr. Thomas Parran Jr., by now the Surgeon General. I do not remember his entire speech, but I know he mentioned the word "venereal" once or twice. I remember this distinctly because I had heard the same word a couple of hours previously, used as a plural noun. I had better tell you about that.

When I got back to my ship after saying goodby to the Neapolitan girl I went up the gangway, faced aft, saluted the flag, faced amidship, saluted the officer of the deck, and prepared to go below to my bunk. However, my way was stopped by a large, wedge-shaped individual whose exact name escapes me now, although it was something like Broadaxe Knoblocker, BM 1/C. The initials stand for Boatswain's Mate, First Class. Knoblocker, who was assisting the officer of the deck, removed four enormous white pills from a cardboard carton and dropped them into my hand. "Eat 'um," he said.

I knew what they were. They were sulfa pills, which had then come into widespread use in the armed forces. "But I don't need them, Boats," I said. "I talked to a girl, sure, but I didn't—"

Knoblocker had the turn of phrase that marks a true BM 1/C. "You are as full of s - - - as an 80-pound robin," he said. "Eat 'um."

"Really, I didn't—"

"Eat 'um, goddammit. Everybody who goes ashore in Naples, he eats the pills when he comes back. You people

ain't going to bring no venereals aboard this ship."

"But I wasn't *exposed* to any venereals, Boats. I only—"

Knoblocker seemed to be getting tense. "I don't care if you was a hundred-year-old eunuch, which you don't look like to me, sailor," he said. "Are you going to eat these delicious pills, or ain't you going to eat these delicious pills?"

Just to please Knoblocker I ate the pills. I later heard that Knoblocker made the *chaplain* eat the pills, too, when the chaplain returned from visiting the church of San Domenico Maggiore, rich in Renaissance sculpture, and the neighboring monastery where the monks point out the cell of St. Thomas Aquinas.

This Knoblocker was a very unspiritual man who had, in Kipling's words, a heathen heart that put its trust in reeking tube and iron shard—particularly in nine reeking triple-mounted six-inch tubes in armored turrets that could throw shards about 15 miles. When those guns went off in full salvo with a concussion that seemed likely to drive a man's kidneys right out through his nostrils, Knoblocker would look around with a rapturous smile as though he heard from somewhere a voice whispering, "Hit 'um again, Boats!"

It must be said that Knoblocker—or rather, the medical officer and the captain—had a point with the pills. Naples was crawling with the venereals at the time, a particularly virulent strain of the venereals that neither German medicine nor American medicine was particularly effective against.

When the Germans departed from Naples they left a colossal booby trap in the post office, a bomb that must have been the size of an interstate moving van, which exploded a long time after they had gone. Many people think

that was the biggest booby trap the Germans left, but it wasn't. The biggest was that dreadful, resistant strain of the venereals. After the Allies captured Naples they naturally did some rejoicing, and pretty soon thousands of soldiers were down with disease, casualties removed from combat as effectively as the Germans might have done with iron shards. So in retrospect the Navy's ounce of prevention, which is about what those four pills weighed, seems a good idea. I sometimes wonder what would have happened if Broadaxe Knoblocker's old mother had come hobbling up the gangplank in her lace shawl. Well, actually I don't wonder—I *know*. "Here, mother," he would have said. "Eat 'um."

The point of my remarks about the Italian girl and old Broadaxe is that by the time we all became entangled in the war, there were only a few isolated people who had not heard about sex and only a few who still tried to suppress the news. Indeed, as early as 1936 FORTUNE had made a survey of thousands of college students and had found that their primary topic of conversation was no longer sex. It was economics. People were hungry. "As for sex," FORTUNE said, "it is, of course, still with us. But the campus takes it more casually than it did … . Sex is no longer news. And the fact that it is no longer news is news."

I did not enter college until 1937, a year after FORTUNE's study, but all my classmates and I were conscious of what FORTUNE had found. It was really a humdinger of a survey: no other magazine had ever attempted to inquire into collegiate opinion in such depth, or done so well at it. Nonetheless, it was with a somewhat heavy heart that I matriculated. Was it true that for the next four years the other 2,600 men

at Princeton were going to talk mostly about fiscal and monetary policy? So it appeared. My roommate, a nice fellow named Horace Graham, eyed me soberly and said, "Are you economically a Keynesian, or do you tend to side more with Raymond Moley?" Then he took a big bite out of a bacon bun.

Somehow, Horace and I managed to get several weeks into the fall term of freshman year talking about such matters until, one desperate evening, we turned on the old At-water Kent to find out what was on. Mae West was on, as a guest on the Chase & Sanborn program on NBC, and she was telling a little story from the Bible, which she had adapted for the airwaves. Miss West was—still is—a clever woman and she wrote a good deal of her own material. It wasn't really dirty; it only sounded dirty because of the way she delivered it. Her story for Chase & Sanborn was about Adam and Eve. In Miss West's version, from which a couple of quotes will suffice here, Eve said, "You've got to stop laying around loafing, Adam. It's time to turn over a new leaf."

To this Adam replied, "I don't care a fig if I do."

Well, next morning there was hell to pay all up and down the country, from pine to palm, apple to orange. Newspapers came out with editorials titled "Mae West Pollutes Homes," and NBC got so rattled that its executives went out and did a good deed—they hastened to sign up the great conductor, Arturo Toscanini, in the hope that his music would somehow clean up all those dirty kilocycles and megacycles that were drifting around in the atmosphere.

While Miss West was making her innocent remarks my roommate, Horace, snorted in an indecent way and I realized that *he* knew about sex, too, and could see some humor in it. When the program was over we fell to talking, and it turned out that both of us had been reluctant to mention sex, all term, because we had thought we should be talking about economics and did not want to appear lowbrow.

Crumbling of Victorian Verities

This belief, we discovered, had been shared by several men in our dormitory. Once the truth was out, however, we talked about sex a whole lot. We didn't practice it much, if that's the word. Princeton was then an all-male university, and the few girls who lived in town were fleet as antelopes. But we did talk, and sometimes we would refer wistfully to the FORTUNE survey to read about how girls lived in the all-female colleges:

"Bull sessions on religion and sex are for more secluded moments. They are more frequent during freshman and sophomore years; upper-class girl students have too much work to do, have talked themselves out with their really good friends, and have discovered the advantages of getting enough sleep . . . . In the evening the girl student may go to the movies, but more often she retires to her room (she likes to live alone) or goes visiting. Late in the evening she makes tea (cocoa is no longer the midnight staple) and spreads some biscuits with jam."

Information of that sort could be a little discouraging. If, by the end of sophomore year, the girls had already talked out everything they knew about sex, there were going to be a lot of frantic midnight calls for the police when, say, the Vassar class of 1941 got married.

On the other hand, sometimes late in the evening I would look across the squalor of our room at my friend Horace. He wasn't making any tea or cocoa or spreading any biscuits with jam. He was just sitting there in his underwear, his feet up on the bookcase, drinking beer straight out of a can and occasionally belching. The sight made me wish I was at Vassar after all.

In its section on the moral code of college students, FORTUNE observed that "the undergraduate, both male and female, seems to be fashioning one without the aid of institutional religion. Ten years ago sexual promiscuity was either a fact or an idea that haunted the imagination. The backwash of war [Note: "war" in this case means one of the other great crowd-pleasers of our century, World War I] and the crumbling of the Victorian verities threw a generation into wild experiment . . . but if the present-day undergraduate indulges in intercourse before marriage with any frequency he doesn't talk much about it . . . the code seems to indicate: reasonable restraint, particularly on the part of the girls, before marriage, and fidelity on both sides after marriage. The only place where the premarital double-standard idea seems to have any popularity is at Pacific Coast universities that are under the Hollywood influence. And the jazz-age experimental attitude still persists, or lingers, on the Coast. Contraceptive knowledge is widespread, and the male undergraduate knows that contraceptive devices can be bought at filling stations. Hence, whether he uses the knowledge for practical purposes or whether he merely reassures himself for a distant future, a shadow has been lifted from his mind."

Not long after we re-read this passage from FORTUNE Horace said to me, "It's a nice day. Why don't we take a walk?"

"Fine," I said. "Where to?"

"Well, I thought maybe we might wander down the back road past Al's Garage, and—"

"Great idea," I said. I knew exactly how he felt. He was a virgin, and so was I, but we both hoped that some day we would get to some exotic part of the world, like Naples, and we needed reassurance for a distant future.

Al was busy in his filling station, misadjusting the timing of a Chevrolet that had been left there for an oil change, so that next week he would have some more business. Horace was a rather shy young man, so it was up to me to begin the conversation. "I can see, Al, that you sell gasoline," I said.

Al didn't say anything, just looked at me.

"I suppose," I said, "I suppose you also sell oil."

"That is pretty good supposing, for a college man," Al said.

"I—ah—I, well, do you sell other things, too?"

Al looked at me silently again.

"I mean—ah—some kind of product that would make a man feel reassured, if he knew he could get it here?"

"What the hell are you talking about? Fan belts?"

I couldn't think of anything else to say, so Horace and I walked on down the road with shadows still on our minds. In the normal course of time and events these shadows disappeared.

As I mentioned a few paragraphs ago, there did remain a few individuals who still attempted to suppress news of sex, and perhaps I had better report on their activities. One would-be suppressor was Frank C. Walker, Postmaster General of the United States, who in 1943 tried, on moral grounds, to revoke *Esquire's* second-class mailing privilege. The magazine still had its Petty girls and, by then, it also had some dandies by a Peruvian-born artist, Alberto Vargas, who signed his work simply, "Varga."

The magazine also printed jokes that were thought by some to be in poor taste. The lawyer for the Post Office Department placed various clergymen on the stand in his case against *Esquire*, and showed the reverend gentlemen various drawings and read them some seamy gags. Were they not lewd and disgusting? Yes, sir, said the clergymen.

Esquire's defense attorney then ambled to the stand, holding a magazine, and showed one of the witnesses a picture of a female nude. The witness, shocked, said he found it sexually stimulating, whereupon the lawyer turned the magazine's cover. It was a copy of *Ladies' Home Journal*.

Esquire's defense attorney then read a joke to another witness, a wartime joke so old that it may seem new to the present generation. It concerned two London charwomen who were discussing the inconveniences of a blackout. "It's a necessary evil," one of them said, "else we're likely to be blasted into maternity."

Said the other, "Aye, but the worst of it is, we'd never know who done it."

The witness found the joke "morally objectionable." *Esquire's* lawyer, with a sly smile, completed the demolition of the Post Office's case. The joke, he pointed out, had been taken from *Reader's Digest*.

Short, Black and Very Smart

Perhaps the most interesting worker in the field of sex-suppression was Father Divine. Father Divine did not say that he was God but on the other hand he did not say he wasn't. What he said was, "If people believe I'm God, then I'm God to them." Father used to carry a brown paper bag full of cash, which, during the Depression, was what many thought God might do.

Father was short, black and very smart. He was able to persuade people to give him money. He had a $28,000 Duesenberg and his secretary had a Rolls-Royce. People would work hard all week and on Saturday they would give him the money. They deeded him their homes and businesses; they gave him all they had. In return, Father operated some dormitories and dining rooms that he called Heavens. He used to serve roast pig. At the height of his career he had a Heaven at Crum Elbow on the Hudson River across from President Roosevelt's house at Hyde Park. He also had branch Heavens in Newark, Baltimore, Detroit, Jersey City, Chicago, Los Angeles and Philadelphia, among other cities, and he numbered uncounted thousands in his flock.

As to sex, Father Divine often spoke out against it. He made all the men live in male dormitories and all the women in female dormitories, and he condemned "lust and passion and all those detestable tendencies." But it happened—indeed, perhaps you have been foreseeing something like this —it happened that one of Father Divine's assistants, whose name was Faithful Mary, got into a misunderstanding with him about money. And Faithful Mary publicly said, "Now the spirit tells me it is time to reveal that Father Divine had affairs with many of the good-looking women in his kingdom. ....The women thought of them as blessings. They thought they had reached the highest peak of virtue when they submitted to Father Divine . . . . He told all the women it was sinful to be with their husbands, but he told them also that they should come to him."

It happened, as well, that a married couple named Rebecca Grace Brown and Onward Universe Brown were not able to live in Father Divine's dormitories. They worked as domestic help in Forest Hills, Long Island, where their employer furnished them with board, room and a double bed. I dare say you are anticipating me again. Although Rebecca Grace and Onward Universe tried hard to keep Father Divine's teachings in mind, the double bed was a problem. Onward would make a detestable proposal to his wife, you know, and then they would lose another battle against sin. On their day off, when they would go to Father Divine's to give him their wages, Father would fix them with an accusing stare and he would say, "I see you have sinned. You cannot hide from God. I am everywhere. I see all. I know all."

Conceivably you might not believe this if you did not have my assurance that I am quoting from public records. And please do not take lightly the memory of Father D. At his death in 1965, the cult's property was valued at more than $10 million, including holdings in New York, New Jersey, Philadelphia, Chicago and on the West Coast.

I scarcely know how to continue. When I originally agreed to write this little book, the editors made me promise to put in something about the orgone box. At that time I had forgotten exactly what the orgone box was. After refreshing my memory, I pleaded with the editors not to make me write about the thing, but they would not take "no" for an answer. The man who invented the orgone box, Dr. Wilhelm Reich, was arrested, and I hardly know how to escape arrest myself.

Dr. Reich was an Austrian psychoanalyst who for six years during the '20s was director of the Vienna Seminar for Psychoanalytic Therapy at the Polyclinic Institute headed by his close associate, Dr. Sigmund Freud. These are excellent credentials, and when Dr. Reich emigrated to the U.S. in 1939 he found a good many doctors and other educated people willing to take seriously his orgone theory.

The doctor believed that the source of the climax in human

sexual activity is something called orgone energy, which is a little like atomic energy. However, orgone energy is not merely erotic in nature. It is "the cosmic life energy" and is found throughout the universe. It is blue in color; the sky is full of it, and it is constantly flowing through everything and everybody. When there is sufficient orgone energy in an individual, his sex life is superlative and he will be less likely to suffer from colds, peptic ulcers, alcoholism, epilepsy, cancer, high blood pressure, obesity and emotional plague, to mention only a few nuisances.

The problem is that most people have too little orgone energy and their sex lives are no fun at all. Dr. Reich's solution was the orgone box, or more properly, the Orgone Energy Accumulator (Pat. Appl. No. 377,277). His model was made of wood, lined with sheet metal, and was just big enough to hold someone seated on a small chair. It looked like an outhouse for small people who were afraid of being shot at.

According to the patent application, organic material such as wood "attracts orgone and absorbs it" whereas "metallic material, especially iron, also attracts orgone, but repels it again rapidly." Thus, if a fellow could just make a pine box lined with boiler plate, orgone energy would be attracted to it from near and far. Dr. Reich calculated that "the concentration of energy inside the accumulator would be about five times the atmospheric concentration." Great good would result if a fellow sat inside that box, lightly clad, absorbing orgone as it ricocheted off the metal lining. Sittings of only 10 to 30 minutes a day would resolve all his problems.

You may think I am getting unreliable. I am not. At one time there were about 50 licensed physicians in the New York area alone practicing what they called orgonomy. One psychiatrist, a professor at Columbia University, called the

orgone box "the most important single discovery in the history of medicine, bar none." There were about 100 orgone boxes in use at one time and these, of course, were only the official boxes. Upon reading about Dr. Reich's idea, a good many enterprising Americans built their own boxes without telling him. This explains the number of old, metal-lined dog houses one sees in back yards today.

Eventually the U.S. Government, through the Food and Drug Administration, blew the whistle on Dr. Reich. He had a theory that he might be able to help cancer sufferers by putting them in orgone boxes. The FDA thought this was a dangerous idea and got a court to enjoin Reich from making and distributing orgone boxes and from issuing printed material alleging that they had therapeutic effects.

Age of the Numbers Game

Reich refused to obey the injunction, refused to plead guilty when brought to trial and demanded a jury of his scientific peers. The court said it had no powers to summon such a jury. It did summon an ordinary jury, which convicted him of criminal contempt, and he was sentenced to a term in the Federal penitentiary at Lewisburg, Pa., where he died in 1957.

There is something quite sad about Dr. Reich's story. It goes beyond the obvious distress one feels at the spectacle of a once-brilliant man who develops a disastrous quirk and ends his days in jail. The larger sadness lies in the notion that any number of people could think there is some scientific secret about sex, or that sex is a sort of numbers game. In 1948 Dr. Alfred Kinsey published his book, *Sexual Behavior in the Human Male*, and I read it with interest, coupled with a vague discomfort that I couldn't quite identify. So I telephoned my old friend Ethel and asked what *she* thought of the book. Ethel said she was willing to believe that 85% of the total U.S. male population has premarital intercourse and that nearly 70% has relations with whores and that Dr. Kinsey and his researchers had interviewed 12,214 people to discover these and other facts. "But they don't make it sound like an awful lot of fun, do they?" Ethel said, and I felt the shock of her essential rightness just as I had felt it long ago on that street corner in Brooklyn.

At about the time Kinsey's book appeared, Boston's Watch and Ward Society said that Kathleen Winsor's dreadful novel, *Forever Amber*, should be banned in Boston. The prosecutor got up before the judge and, yelling a little, said the book contained 70 references to sexual intercourse, 39 illegitimate pregnancies, seven abortions and 33 bedroom scenes "more or less sexual." The judge looked bored, and he ruled that the book could be sold in Boston because, "while conducive to sleep, it is not conducive to a desire to sleep with a member of the opposite sex." Perhaps it was just around that moment that the Swing Era cooled off and began to draw toward its close. So many people had begun to think and talk about sex in arithmetical terms that they had temporarily forgotten what it is really about, and that it does not begin on page 472, graph six, chart two, but on an April afternoon when the world and you are young.   — ROBERT WALLACE

Whitney Darrow, Jr.

Gene Krupa

On his platform above the rest of the band, the drummer chomps his gum, tosses his curly black hair, twirls his sticks and begins one of the most incredible performances of the Swing Era. He rears back in soulful appreciation of a swinging beat, bends low over the tom-toms as if in intimate conversation and whirls from cymbal to snare to tom-tom in a cyclone of rolls, flams, paradiddles and ratamacues. Listeners closest to the band may be able to hear him shout above the uproar, "Lyonnaise potatoes and some pork chops!" Gene Krupa is off on one of the solos that make swing fans bounce and yell and applaud as they do for Harry James's agile trumpet or Benny Goodman's darting clarinet.

Long before crowds rocked to the spectacle of Gene Krupa "grunting and sweating like I was in a steel mill," as he once described himself, there had been virtuoso jazz drummers. Krupa learned his art from—and gratefully acknowledged his debt to—men like Baby Dodds, Zutty Singleton and Chick Webb. But no other drummer of the Swing Era had the advantage of being showcased by the most popular of all swing bands—Benny Goodman's—along with the skill, the jazz feeling and the showmanship needed to establish the drums in the public mind as a vital and visible component of swing and an instrument unequaled as a show in itself.

The drummer has a natural edge as a crowd-pleaser. His tools look spectacular, create a wider range of sounds than any other instrument and can be heard above the loudest horns. Krupa has always made full use of all these assets. He has also provided something much more important to musicians though seldom apparent to most listeners—the steady, driving beat that lifts and propels a band.

Of all the instruments in swing, the drums are perhaps the most closely related to the African music that is one of the wellsprings of jazz, and jazz, originally a black man's art, produced many superb drummers. Some of them were on display in the Chicago of the '20s when Krupa was growing up there, and they provided him with as good a background as any drummer could have wished.

Gene was born in Chicago on Jan. 15, 1909, youngest of the nine children of Bartley and Ann Krupa. Both of Gene's parents were of Polish descent. His father and his mother's

parents were all natives of Poland; Ann Krupa was born in Pennsylvania. "My father died pretty early," says Gene, "and my mother, who was a milliner, had to work hard to bring all these kids up right." The children went to work as soon as they could—Gene at eleven.

"My brother Pete worked in the Brown Music Company," he says, "and he got me a gig as a chore boy around the store—dust the pianos, run errands, wash windows. On busy days they'd let me sell records and demonstrate piano rolls. I used to look in their wholesale catalogue for a musical instrument—piano, trombone, cornet—I didn't care what it was as long as it was an instrument. The cheapest item was the drums, 16 beans, I think, for a set of Japanese drums; a great high, wide bass drum, with a brass cymbal on it, a wood block and a snare drum."

Gene, the only really musical Krupa, scraped up "16 beans" and bought the set. "It became my life immediately," he says. But learning to play was easier than finding somebody to play with. "Guys were out having gang wars, hitting each other with rocks. Mostly it would have to be a

girl to play the piano. Playing with a saxophone or something like that, my goodness, that was like impossible. Where would you find a guy that played the saxophone?"

Gene found some, finally, when he got into school bands and played for "socials," which led to a few dates for real money and membership in the American Musicians Union. "The AMU was an apprenticeship to join the Fed [American Federation of Musicians]," he says. "AMU guys played the rougher, cheaper jobs, but they were more talented in jazz. You'd go down on Saturdays, try to pick up what gigs you could for the week, and chat with the guys. One guy much older than I was, quite a good drummer by the name of Al Silverman, would tell me about drummers who were legends even to him—Baby Dodds, George Wettling, Davey Tough."

Krupa finally got to hear some of these legends. "That was something else," he says reverently. His AMU friends could see that Gene belonged in the big leagues, too, and prodded him to join the "Fed."

"Finally I went up there and took their big test," he says.

On a Sunday outing, Gene, age 7, holds down the sidecar while his brother Julius confidently mans the controls. The motorcycle belonged to their elder brother Pete, a phonograph repairman who later got Gene his first job—as a music-store chore boy.

"The guy said, 'Make a roll. That's it. Give us 50 bucks. You're in.'" As a union member he got jobs "with bands like the Hoosier Bellhops and Eddie Mulhaney's Red Jackets, playing this Mickey Mouse music to make bread."

At least, playing with Mickey Mouse bands was less risky than Gene's earlier job at Wagner's Hall in a South Chicago area called The Bush. "Boy, if you got caught around there just minding your own business, you were in danger," he remembers. "The gig was from 8 o'clock Saturday until midnight. Come 11 o'clock, the fight would start. Factions chose up against each other and started swinging. At closing time, the fight would still be going on, but I became sort of a favorite of these kids. I'd move my drums to the edge of the stage, so I could get them off. And some cat, some real mean guy who was one of the gang leaders, would give a shrill whistle and they'd stop and clear a path for me. Start swinging again as soon as I left."

Drumming filled Gene's mind; his high-school grades suffered. His family nagged him. "They looked down on musicians and thought I was a bum." To please his mother, who hoped he might become a priest, Gene spent a year at a seminary, St. Joseph's College, and studied harder than usual—then he went back to the drums full time.

Soon came a memorable day: "Davey Tough came up to me and said, 'I hear you play pretty nice.' Bashful, I said, 'Yes, can I hear you play sometime?' Davey said, 'Gee, if you think I can play, you ought to hear Baby Dodds.' And he took me down to Kelly's Stable.

"It's hard to describe how fantastic Baby was. He was terrific on rim shots and the standard cymbal beat we carry most of the time now, but he saved that for maybe just the last eight bars—what we call a rideout. The number would be mostly played on the snare drum, which was the style then, like parade drums, almost military. Then right before going to the cymbal for that rideout, he would get into this press roll, dragging the sticks across the drum, and that was something else. The place would start to rock."

Gene began going regularly to hear Dodds, drummer Zutty Singleton, trumpeter Louis Armstrong and pianist Earl Hines. "All our gigs ended at 12 o'clock; these guys would work until two or three in the morning. We'd go out and listen to them all night. Any idea that I knew anything about the skins had to go out the window once I started visiting those South Side joints. I had no idea of the wide range of effects you could get from a set of drums. I picked up from Zutty and Baby the difference between starting a roll, or a sequence of beats, with the left or right hand and how the tone and inflection is changed entirely when you shift hands. Those Negro drummers did it as nonchalantly as though it were a game.

"I next went to work on the tom-toms, trying to get them in tune and knowing when to use 'em. I punched holes in the heads with an ice pick, as Zutty had told me, until they were pitched just right. Another trick I got from Baby was how to keep the bass and snare drum in tune and how to get cymbals that rang in tune. Most white musicians of that day thought drums were something to beat hell out of. Few of them realized that drums have a broad range of tonal variations."

Gene was getting better known now and was asked to play at the Rendezvous in downtown Chicago with a band that included clarinetist Mezz Mezzrow, pianist Joe Sullivan and trombonist Floyd O'Brien—giants in Gene's world. "It was the first time I'd ever played with a bass, not a string bass but a bass tuba—that's how far back this goes," says Gene. "You can't imagine what a feeling that was. And with all these big-time players around me, and liking me, wow! Your fondest dreams come true!"

Besides playing at the Rendezvous, Gene joined in jam sessions at the Three Deuces on State Street, a favorite hangout of musicians. There, in a dismal downstairs room, he played through many nights and often past dawn with Chicago musicians like clarinetists Frank Teschemacher and Benny Goodman, Benny's bassist brother Harry, saxophonist Bud Freeman and banjoist Eddie Condon, and with visitors like cornetist Bix Beiderbecke, the Dorsey brothers and Glenn Miller.

When Davey Tough left for Europe, Gene replaced him in the loosely organized group that included Teschemacher, Freeman, Condon, Sullivan, cornetist Jimmy McPartland and bassist Jim Lannigan. "Eddie Condon found him," Bud Freeman remembers. "Gene was the first drummer we could find who would fit in with what we wanted to do."

Krupa, who at that time could not read a note of music, was learning everything by ear. "We were emulating the guys at Kelly's Stable, trying to emulate Louis Armstrong," he says, "and I'd say that's how the Chicago style was born."

At one of its jam sessions the group impressed Red McKenzie who had come from St. Louis to scout for musicians for his Mound City Blue Blowers. He persuaded Tommy Rockwell of OKeh Records to let the youngsters cut a couple of sides. The group that showed up at OKeh's barnlike studio at 10 a.m. on Dec. 9, 1927, was christened the McKenzie-Condon Chicagoans for the occasion and included Teschemacher on clarinet, Freeman on tenor sax, McPartland on cornet, Lannigan on bass and tuba, Sullivan on piano, Condon on banjo and Gene Krupa on drums.

Like a Triple Bourbon

As Condon tells it in his book, *We Called It Music*, Krupa was setting up his drums when Rockwell strolled over. " 'What are you going to do with those?' Rockwell asked. 'Play them,' Krupa said simply. Rockwell shook his head. 'You'll ruin our equipment; all we've ever used are snare drums and cymbals.' Krupa, who'd been practicing every day at home, looked crushed. 'How about letting us try them?' I asked. 'The drums are the backbone of the band. They hold us up.' Rockwell was leery. " 'All right, but

I'm afraid the bass drum and those tom-toms will knock the needle off the wax and into the street.' "

The band prepared to make the first recordings ever of a bass drum and of Gene Krupa. "I gave the boys the beat, and we jumped into *China Boy*," says Condon. "The nights and years of playing in cellars and saloons and ballrooms, of practicing separately and together, of listening to Louis and Joe Oliver and Jimmie Noone and Leon Rappolo, of losing sleep and breathing bad air and drinking licorice gin paid off. We were together and apart at the same time. . . . Krupa's drums went through us like a shot of triple bourbon."

The needle stayed on the wax. The Chicagoans cut *China Boy*, *Sugar* and, a couple of weeks later, *Liza* and *Nobody's Sweetheart*. Gene's drums are evident in the background on those old records as a steady, propulsive force. Teschemacher's clarinet, McPartland's cornet and Freeman's sax are fresh and inventive. The records, when released in 1928, "made quite a lot of noise among the musicians in New York," says Gene. "They said, 'Hey, what are these kids doing?' " The kids were doing something new.

Chicago jazz was on its way. The Chicagoans arrived in New York a few months after their recording session all set

Gene checks the music while Benny Goodman adjusts the mouthpiece of his clarinet during rehearsals for the 1937 film Hollywood Hotel. *While with the Goodman band Gene also played in* The Big Broadcast of 1937. *He has since appeared in a score of films but prefers to work with live audiences. "I enjoyed doing movies," he says, "but I wouldn't want to do them all the time."*

to accompany singer Bea Palmer who had a job at the Chateau Madrid nightclub. Their prospective employer loved Bea but hated the band. No job.

"We went into a big panic," says Gene. "But we had the respect of the Dorseys, Bix, all those guys; and they were feeding us, throwing a little bit our way when they could."

"Bea was taking us to parties," Condon recalls. "Musicians came to see us and brought liquor, but never food. When you're broke you can get all the whisky you want, but don't ask for a sandwich; it lowers the social tone of the friendship.

"At first, the only place we could play was in our rooms at our own request. Krupa set up his drums, and we played every night." Among the musicians who dropped in to listen, says Condon, was Vic Berton, one of the established New York drummers. "When we saw Vic listening with admiration to Krupa, our faith in our future rose."

The Chicagoans had plenty of time to go to Harlem and listen to the great black musicians playing there, just as they had listened to the black bands on Chicago's South Side, and Bud Freeman, among others, thinks that their example made white New York musicians Harlem-conscious, too. Whoever discovered Harlem, all musicians enjoyed it.

"There was a constant search for a new kind of music," says Gene, "and it was important to listen to everyone—Fats Waller, Zutty, Tatum, Louis, Willie 'The Lion' Smith, Chick Webb—no matter what the instrument or the style. I always felt like going uptown was taking a lesson.

Ride on a High-Hat

"We sat in with all the bands. I learned practically *everything* from Chick; he gave me a whole new picture of drums. He was cleaner, faster and more technical than most of the other drummers. Chick was one of the first I heard use sticks on the high-hat cymbal [two cymbals mounted so that they can be clapped together by a foot pedal]. Most guys were using the cymbals that were at floor level and too low to use your sticks on. He had the high-hat going all the time, and he used real thin sticks, long and light. He played a lot on the snare drum, and he had that bass drum going all the time. Before I got to know Chick, I was more on a small band kick, the Chicago-style offshoot of Dixieland. Chick brought out the more modern band kick.

"Chicago drumming was rawer, more primitive than the New York style. Even Sonny Greer, playing with Ellington, had become rather sophisticated. Drummers like Vic Berton were playing mostly on the cymbals with little tricks underneath them. We Chicago guys were playing more on the snare drums and tom-toms. The first New York job I had, Red Nichols hired me to play in the Hollywood Restaurant, where they had a chorus line doing a Samoan number. That's all I had to see and I'm immediately playing on the tom-toms. Those girls went crazy. And talk started going around town. 'We don't know what that kid's doing,' they'd say, 'but he's sure making that show.' It was kind of a mixed-up scene because we were trying to copy the New York guys and they were trying to copy us."

Like Gene, the other members of the Chicagoans were getting jobs with various bands. The group ceased to exist as a unit, though members of it often met in recording studios, always with entertaining results.

Gene went with the Nichols band from the Hollywood Restaurant into the Times Square Theater to play for George Gershwin's 1930 musical, *Strike Up the Band*. Benny Goodman was in that pit band and so was Glenn Miller. Fortunately for Gene, who still couldn't read music, Miller sat right in front of Krupa. "I couldn't tell a quarter note from an eighth note. Every time we got something new," says Gene, "I'd pass my part up to Glenn, who'd sort of hum the rhythm for me till I got it into my head."

Even though he couldn't read music, Gene impressed Gershwin by introducing him to the "freeze beat." Some arranger had added to Gershwin's score a four-bar solo on temple blocks. Gene, who "used to get sick to my stomach when I saw temple blocks," told the composer: "Mr. Gershwin, they're corny; you don't use temple blocks."

"What do you do?" asked Gershwin.

Gene remembered a device he'd seen used in Cotton Club shows with Duke Ellington's band. He said: "You have everyone onstage come to a dead stop for a few seconds." This freeze beat, a sudden pause now commonly used to focus an audience's attention on a stage scene or a piece of music, was a novelty on Broadway then. "It stopped the show," says Gene. "When I got my own band, we used the same stop in our big hit, *Leave Us Leap*." When Nichols began organizing a band later that year for Gershwin's next show, *Girl Crazy*, the composer asked Nichols to include Krupa.

While Gene was in the lineup his strong drumming helped the Nichols band to make some of its best records, sides like *I Want To Be Happy*, *Sheik of Araby*, *Carolina in the Morning* and *Dinah*.

When *Girl Crazy* closed in 1931, Gene joined the band Benny Goodman had organized for crooner Russ Colombo, which included Jimmy McPartland, Joe Sullivan and Harry Goodman, and played a lot of theater dates. "I rounded myself out as a percussionist," says Gene. "I played everything, vibraphone, timpani, chimes." He also finally learned to read music and studied drumming with Sanford Moeller, a highly respected drummer turned teacher. Moeller favored an up-and-down style of drumming, with lots of arm movement, which Gene still uses, combining flailing arms with powerful wrists and fingers to produce an awesome volume of sound.

After the Colombo band broke up in 1932, Gene worked for a couple of years in the commercial bands of Irving Aaronson, Horace Heidt and Mal Hallet to "make enough money to go out at night and jam someplace with the bands and guys you wanted to play with." And also enough to support his bride, Ethel Fawcett, whom he had met while staying at Manhattan's Dixie Hotel where she was a telephone operator. They got married in June 1933, a rugged time for musicians. Late one night, Eddie Condon and Max Kaminsky were thrown out of their rooms for nonpayment of rent. They began calling friends. When

Sweat-soaked but ecstatic, Gene whirls his wire brushes and shouts exuberantly during the historic "battle" staged on May 4, 1937, at Harlem's Savoy Ballroom between the bands of Benny Goodman and Chick Webb. Bassist Harry Goodman (left) plunks soulfully and a young Harry James grins engagingly. An overflow crowd jammed the ballroom; some fans even climbed up on the bandstand with the musicians. Although Chick seldom lost a decision at the Savoy, where his group was house band, he exerted a special effort for this encounter. And it was not until the room had rocked for four hours to the rhythmic offerings of both bands that the crowd finally gave Chick the edge. "I've never been cut by a better man," conceded Gene cheerfully.

they reached Gene, he said, "Come right down. I'm sorry we haven't a better place, but this is all we could find." Says Kaminsky: "We discovered later that it was his wedding night."

In 1934 Gene joined the band of movie star Buddy Rogers who so fancied himself as a musician that he liked to play all the instruments in his 16-man outfit. His drum solo failed to impress Krupa. After the first show the man who had shown Gershwin the freeze beat went to Rogers' dressing room.

"Now, this guy is busy with a million things—chicks, interviewers, radio guys—and I say, 'Can I see you a minute? Look, Mr. Rogers, if you're going to do that drum solo, let me teach you a decent 16 bars.' Rogers turns purple and shouts, 'OUT!' He asks the manager, 'Who *is* that fresh kid?' But the manager managed to pacify him, said I was drum mad, and Rogers decided to put up with me."

While Rogers was putting up with Krupa, Benny Goodman, back in New York, had organized a band to play on a radio program sponsored by the National Biscuit Company, which was launching a new product, the "RITZ" cracker.

"I heard a couple of those broadcasts," says Gene. "Boy, did that band thrill me!"

As Benny remembers it, "The band was shaping up, but it still wasn't anything like the way I wanted it to sound. The rhythm, especially, wasn't right. Our drummer was merely adequate, and a couple of new men we tried didn't seem to add anything. The man I really wanted, Gene Krupa, was out in Chicago, playing with Buddy Rogers.

"John Hammond . . . went to Chicago to try to corral Krupa. He happened to hit Gene on a night when Rogers, who was versatile but not much of a jazzman, was working out on about eleven different instruments. Gene was having a sad time but for various reasons didn't want to change jobs.

" 'This is going to be a real jazz band,' John urged. 'Think of the kicks.'

"About then Buddy Rogers picked up another instrument and prepared for a solo.

" 'I'll come,' Gene said."

Whale of a Difference

According to Gene, Hammond added some even more persuasive points. "He told me, 'You'll work one day a week, Saturday night. You do two three-hour broadcasts—one for the East Coast, one for the West Coast.' That's it and the money equals what I was getting with Rogers. I realized that it was made to order for me. I could do all the extra gigs, practice and do a lot of studying. So I joined—it was really a thrill."

"All the guys were pretty excited," adds the modest Gene, "because they seemed to think I made a difference to the band."

In his book, *My Life in Jazz*, Max Kaminsky has explained the kind of difference Gene made to that band: "A jazz musician never feels so happy playing as when he's playing with a great drummer. A jazz drummer is a whole percus-sion section in one person. While his right foot is striking the bass drum for the beat and his left is working the high-hat pedal for the afterbeat, his left hand is beating out accents on the snare and his right hand is riding the high-hat or one of the big cymbals or tom-toms. . . . In all music the basics are rhythm, harmony and melody, but in jazz the rhythm is foremost. . . . Gene Krupa actually made Benny Goodman's band."

The jazz drummer's art is indeed a miracle of timing and coordination. He has before him two tom-toms, a bass and a snare and an assortment of cymbals (some drummers have used as many as seven), which he can strike with sticks and wire brushes (or sometimes mallets or just his hands) to produce dozens of different kinds of sounds. The number of different possible combinations of these sounds in all their shadings, variations and tempos is virtually infinite.

Some Swing Era drummers further embellished their sets with wood blocks, cowbells and ratchets. Krupa disdains such foofaraw. He has seldom used a cowbell, for instance, except to signal the end of one of his solos.

The drummer must keep all this arsenal of sounds in mind while maintaining a steady beat and playing different accents within this basic tempo, a feat roughly comparable to Julius Caesar's alleged ability to read, write, talk and listen at the same time. The drummer's decibel range in any of these tempos, must extend from ear-shattering booms and crashes to a barely audible rustle. Every sound, however loud or soft, requires skill, technique and effort. And the drummer is seldom idle. The pianist pauses, the sax section lays out for 32 measures, the brass takes a rest—but the drummer is always there, supplying the pulse without which the whole process stops. And he must constantly adapt to all the rest of the band. "The truly great drummer," says Kaminsky, "knows what to play with all the different solos."

Most Swing Era drummers finished every night's work wringing wet. Some of the greatest of them (Chick Webb, Davey Tough) were so small and seemed so frail that every performance was like a miracle. Krupa stands only 5 ft. 7½ in., but with his broad shoulders and wide, muscular callused hands, he looks almost as powerful as he sounds. He has never needed to take any exercise, beyond drumming, to keep in shape.

His *extensor carpi radiali*, the muscles just above the wrist on the inside of his forearm, are abnormally developed from the constant motion of his wrists and hump up astonishingly when he clenches his fist. From gripping the sticks, he has heavy calluses on his right little finger and left middle finger. A manicurist once filed his calluses off when he fell asleep in a barber's chair; he spent painful weeks redeveloping them.

Four months after Krupa joined it, the Goodman band created one of swing's most persistently chronicled legends by nearly expiring on the road and then leaping to fame on Aug. 21, 1935, in the Palomar Ballroom in Los Angeles. The band had truly launched the Swing Era. "But if you think it was clear sailing from then on, you don't know the music

Krupa's band modified its style in 1941 to accommodate the electrifying trumpet of Roy ("Little Jazz") Eldridge and the jazz vocalizing of singer Anita O'Day. They stayed with Krupa until 1943 and helped to produce some of the most popular records the band ever made.

business," says Benny. The band still had to develop a solid style—and a following across the country.

"The band started to get together as we went on the road," says Hymie Shertzer, then Benny's lead alto sax. "A lot of what we did was ad lib, so everyone had a hand in developing the style. That band had a wonderful feeling about it. We had 14 men who all had the same conception of music. The band was so beautifully tuned it was like a fine watch. Gene gave the band a drive, and after a while he really started to become a crowd-puller. So Benny began giving him longer and longer solos."

One of Goodman's biggest hits was *Sing, Sing, Sing,* which started as a short arrangement with vocal and became a 15-minute showcase for Gene.

That Springboard Tune

Gene recalls that Jimmy Mundy, who arranged *Sing, Sing, Sing* as a vocal for Helen Ward, gave him a four-bar introduction. "Benny liked what I did on the intro," he says, "so he suggested I do as much as I wanted and give a signal when I wanted the guys to come in. We never played it the same way twice; I'd do a few little things, then Harry James would come in, then Benny, and after the solos we'd start with collective improvisations. Every night it became a sort of jam session with us.

"There was this thing Benny and I had throughout the years where we could set each other off. We'd be playing good, and all of a sudden one of us would do something—nothing spectacular, certainly nothing the audience would notice, maybe not even the rest of the musicians—but it was like a springboard. Later on, this kind of groove spread out in the trio with Teddy Wilson on the piano, and then the quartet with Lionel Hampton and the vibes. It was like a meeting of minds, and it would touch off something beautiful."

Beautiful indeed are some of the performances Krupa recorded with Goodman. He is intense and driving in *Sing, Sing, Sing,* crisp and clean in *Blue Skies,* and bold and daring in *Swingtime in the Rockies.*

Krupa looked as exciting as he sounded. Fans idolized the whole Goodman band and none more than Krupa. "Gene was always a great showman," says Bud Freeman, "and by that I don't mean to put down his talent. His showmanship was not separate from his talent; there was a oneness. His playing was full of an enthusiasm that was completely sincere. One thing about Gene is he's *real.* And that's what the kids sensed. There was a terrific rapport between them, they identified with him. Gene became the big attraction of the Goodman band. Girls reacted to him the way they did to Frank Sinatra."

"Gene's solos had great visual appeal," says Shertzer. "The crowd saw someone knocking his brains out and they loved it." The crowd also loved the "grunting" that went with his solos. Gene once told critic George Simon he might be muttering "boom-did-dee" for the tune he was playing, "dang" for a rim shot, and "paaah" for a cymbal shot. One of Gene's favorite grunts started one day "when

Autograph hounds besiege Gene in 1940 as sidemen Walter Bates and Shorty Sherock observe. Three years later a narcotics conviction seemed to threaten his career, but Gene came back with another band and the crowds followed. Below, fans line up for his 1944 appearance at the Capitol Theater in New York.

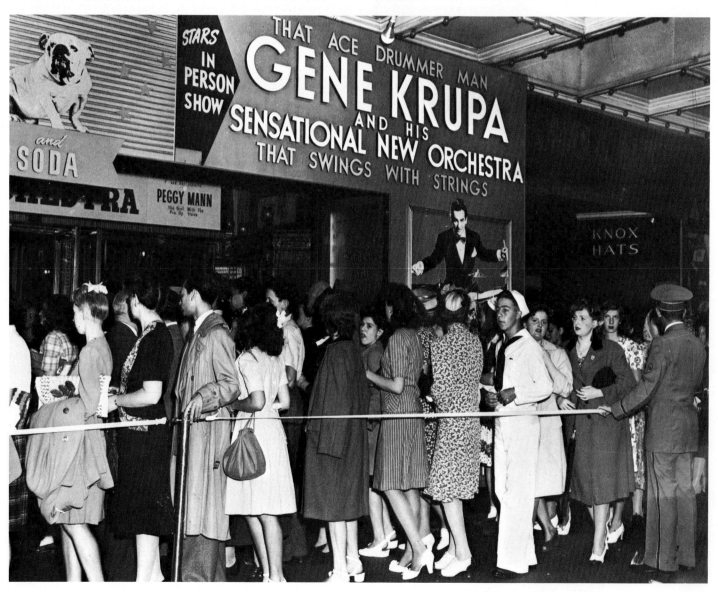

I was hungry for Lyonnaise potatoes and some pork chops. I noticed the phrase had swing, so that night in the band I grunted that."

Many drummers copied Gene; few could top him. Indeed, about the only time he was ever publicly outswung was when Goodman lost a famous battle of the bands to Krupa's old mentor, Chick Webb, at the Savoy Ballroom on May 11, 1937. "Chick really did me up that night," Gene gracefully concedes. "I've never been cut by a better man."

Another great moment for the Goodman band was Carnegie Hall's first jazz concert on Jan. 16, 1938. Goodman was nervous, but not for long: "The shout that went up from the crowd was the same one we'd been hearing in dance halls across the country, and we knew we had them. The noise continued until we played our final number, the 15-minute version of *Sing, Sing, Sing*. During that one people started to dance in the aisles and had to be restrained."

As a first magnitude star, Krupa was under enormous pressure to head his own band. "Managers got hold of all the sidemen," he explains. "They'd say, 'Are you going to own your own store or work as a clerk?' Who doesn't succumb to a thing like that? Also, though I got paid well as a sideman, there's no comparison to what I made on my own. And, of course, I had my own ideas. Benny liked to work everything out, go over and over every number; I lean more toward the improvisational side."

Krupa began preparing to leave Goodman. "I had bookings, record contracts, everything. Success was practically assured right from the start." A few weeks after the Carnegie Hall concert, Krupa and Goodman fell out over some trivial matter, and soon after Gene left the band.

The Krupa band opened on April 16, 1938. Better than 4,000 fans crammed the ballroom at the Steel Pier in Atlantic City, besieging the bandstand and shrieking for more. "Krupa's Band Kills Cats," *Metronome* headlined.

For a while, Gene was more soloist than leader. Of the band's first 70 arrangements, Gene says, "I think 69 of them featured me." One ballroom manager told him, "Gene you're a good kid, a nice boy and a hard worker, but even the *Super Chief* stops once in a while. Don't take so many solos—my ears are hurting."

"Gene did play loud," says trumpeter Shorty Sherock, who sat next to Krupa for a while. "When he hit the cymbal my head would reel. Once he hit the foot pedal on the bass drum so hard he put the mallet right through the drum—took two guys to pull it out."

Guitarist Ray Biondi remembers that it took Gene about six months to work himself up to leading the band and letting somebody else sit in on drums from time to time. He remembers also that Gene sought constantly to improve the band by picking up better sidemen and that he favored black arrangers—"guys like Chappy Willett, Jimmy Mundy, Fred Norman, Benny Carter; he wanted the style that only they could give him."

Tenor saxophonist Sam Donahue, one of the sidemen Gene hired on the road, remembers that band as pleasant and fairly easygoing in life-style and in music. It sounded a lot like the Goodman band—the public admired Benny almost as much as Gene did, and Gene liked to please people. "If someone requested another band's tune," says Donahue, "some leaders would tell them to get their money back. Gene was never that way; he played what the audience wanted."

Because audiences liked commercial bands and lots of ballads, Krupa played lots of ballads and kept his band commercial enough to please most people without sacrificing its ability to swing. He kept up with changes in taste, too. In 1941 the band entered a new era of success with a slightly different style and the additions of trumpeter Roy Eldridge and singer Anita O'Day. Anita wasn't born with that fine old Irish name. Her surname was originally Colton, and she changed it more from whim than anything else. "O'Day" is pig Latin for "dough," and "I wanted some," says Anita. Gene found her singing at his old Chicago hangout, the Three Deuces, and hired her when Irene Day left the band to get married.

Unlike most girl singers of the time, Anita was never coy or cute. "She could sound like a jazz horn," says Krupa. She dispensed with frills even in her clothes, wearing jackets like the rest of the band—to save money, she says. "I made $40 a week; I was lucky to get my shirts out of the laundry. There were no girl vocalist unions in those days." But she loved the job. "I was just a kid on the road, and I was having a ball. I was doing the same thing in Krupa's band that Gene had done in Goodman's band—acquiring a name for myself."

Anita, then Roy, then—Bam!

Roy Eldridge, who has been called "one of the most electrifying trumpeters of all time," was an old friend of Gene's and a man he yearned to have in his lineup. "I dug this guy, dug his playing so much," says Krupa. But Eldridge was doing well with his own group, and the modest Krupa hesitated to suggest a switch. He finally popped the question and was astonished when Roy accepted. The money helped. Eldridge had been making $125 a week with his own black band; in Krupa's white band he got $150.

"I felt that with the coming of Anita and Roy we started to find ourselves, we really started to move," says Gene. Anita and Roy created some of the band's biggest hits. Things like *Thanks for the Boogie Ride* and *That's What You Think* showed off Anita's incomparable jazz technique with or without words. Roy demonstrated his mellow lyric quality in *Rockin' Chair* and his incredible virtuosity in *After You've Gone* in which he plays at frantic speed but clearly articulates every note. In *Let Me Off Uptown*, Roy and Anita exchange amusing patter. Anita says, "It was just a little dialogue over some vamping music. A chorus, some more dialogue, and then the trumpet came in. We did it just like any other piece of material. But within three weeks it had sold a million copies." Well, maybe not a *million*, Anita, but as Gene says, "It was probably our biggest hit."

Roy and Anita both say that their styles developed while they worked with Krupa. Anita, particularly, adapted to fit the band's style. Gene changed his style, too, and though the music continued to be written around the drums, he shared the limelight ungrudgingly with Roy and Anita, whom he calls "a delightful combination" and "the springboard I needed."

The whole Krupa outfit amounted to a mutual admiration society. "He was really wonderful; not a hard man at all," says Sherock. And Eldridge remembers that "Gene never turned or glared at you if you hit a bum note. He just let you play the way you knew best. He never drove you."

Gene was unquestionably the leader of the band (Anita remembers that he was always "Mr. Krupa" to her), but he was also one of the boys. He ate and drank with the sidemen. (Under the pressures of life on the road Gene was becoming a heavy drinker.) He and Ethel gave annual Christmas parties for them. When the band hit Chicago, Gene would take some of them home for a taste of his mother's Polish cooking and then to the South Side to hear the black drummers.

"Gene's band was very stimulating for everybody," says Anita. "That's why we all worked so hard. Why, we'd do seven shows a day. Empty a theater and do it again. Those were great times."

The great times ended in 1943. Before half the year was out Anita had left the band to get married, Gene's wife had divorced him, alleging that she had suffered from his "violent temper" and "extreme cruelty" and Gene himself had landed in jail on a narcotics charge.

The trouble started when Gene's valet was drafted and decided to show Gene how much he had enjoyed working for him by giving him a parting present. Says Gene: "By then I was the glamour boy—15 camel hair coats, three trunks around with me all the time—and he couldn't think what to get me. Finally he thought, 'Gee, I'll get Gene some grass.' At that time, California was hot as a pistol, you could park your car for a bottle of beer and get arrested. So he had a rough time getting the stuff. He probably shot his mouth off a little—'I'm getting this for the greatest guy in the world, Gene Krupa.'"

Gene left the grateful valet's gift at his hotel. Then police, apparently tipped off, searched the theater where the band was playing.

"I suddenly remember the stuff's at the hotel where they're going next," says Gene. "So I call up my new valet and say, 'Send my laundry out. In one of my coats you'll find some

The Krupa Trio—Gene, saxophonist Charlie Ventura and pianist Teddy Napoleon—was formed on the spur of the moment during a recording session, and alternated on the stand with Gene's big band during the late '40s. After Krupa broke up his band in 1951, the Trio—with Flip Phillips replacing Ventura—toured with Gene as part of the Jazz at the Philharmonic series.

cigarettes. Throw them down the toilet.' But the kid puts them in his pocket and the police nail him on the way out, so I get arrested."

Gene hired topflight lawyer Jake Ehrlich, not knowing, he says, that the district attorney disliked Ehrlich. Gene feels that this antagonism helped create the wave of publicity that followed. The case made front pages across the country, often with pictures of Gene being carted off in a paddy wagon. Many teen-agers learned for the first time about the existence of pot. "The papers had me responsible for everything," says Gene. "I was a very conservative dresser, and they blamed me for zoot suits, big key chains and juvenile delinquency."

"If it had been anybody but Gene," says Roy Eldridge, "that case would never have happened."

"The ridiculous thing was that I was such a boozer I never thought about grass," Gene says. "I'd take grass, and it would put me to sleep. I was an out-and-out lush." (Gene has since become a moderate drinker.)

Gene pleaded guilty to the charge of possession, a misdemeanor, and was given 90 days. He was convicted also on a charge of contributing to the delinquency of a minor, a felony. He was finally freed on bail after serving 84 days of the 90-day sentence and went home, to the nine-room house he had built in Yonkers in 1941, to await the outcome of his appeal on the felony conviction.

"Oh, sure, I was mad," he says, "but how long can you stay mad? So long you break out in rashes? Besides, the shock of the whole thing probably helped me. I might have gone on to much worse things. It brought me back to religion."

The Thunder and the Tears

Anyone less solidly poised than Gene might have crumbled. His band was gone; Roy Eldridge had tried vainly to hold it together before giving up and going out on his own again. And nobody seemed to have a job for Gene. Then Goodman telephoned.

"He was one of the few guys who'd come to see me when I was sent up," says Gene. "He said, 'My house isn't far from yours, get in the car and bring your drums.' We had a session at his home, and then I agreed to join his band at the New Yorker Hotel for the ice show. That was fun, you can roll with skaters taking spins. Then Tommy Dorsey said why didn't I try coming down with him at the Paramount."

Gene seized this chance for a comeback but was nervous about his reception, so there was no announcement that he would appear with Dorsey. But fans spotted him when the orchestra rose out of the pit for the first show. Whispers, then clapping, then cheers ran around the theater. At the end of the first number Tommy asked Gene to stand up. The crowd broke into a thunderous ovation and Gene burst into tears.

"The guy treated me like a million," says Gene. "And I taught him something about drumming, too. We were planning a routine and Tommy said, 'Okay, Gene, you play a 16-bar solo in front.' I wanted to know in front of what. Tommy couldn't understand what difference it made. I told him a drummer's got to fit in with what's being played around him.

Gene beats the bongos while Cozy Cole strokes the conga drum as they open a New York drum school together in 1954. Gene, impatient with teaching, soon retired from active participation.

He can't just go soaring off into space. Later he admitted I was absolutely right.

"While with Tommy I developed my 'Kostelanetz' complex. We had a lovely David Rose arrangement of *Sleepy Lagoon*, a very legato arrangement that didn't need any drums. Tommy had a solo in it, so I used to conduct. It had a lot of time-signature changes, and the strings and harp were lovely. I got a big kick out of it." The sound of the strings stayed with Gene; after being acquitted of the felony charge, he left Dorsey and in 1944 formed his own "Band That Swings with Strings."

"We had ten guys in the string section," he says. "I got quite a kick out of having that band, and conducting it, but it was very expensive and very unsuccessful commercially."

Gene traded his swinging strings for a touch of bop. "I'd been digging Diz and Bird and a few of the guys; they sounded pretty nice to me. And we'd gotten Buddy Wise, Don Fagerquist and Dick Taylor into the band. Gerry Mulligan was doing arrangements. We even had Gerry playing for awhile, but the other guys on sax said they'd quit if I didn't get him out of there, because he didn't have command of the instrument then and he was messing up a pretty smooth sax section. Gerry and I had our little problems. He'd come on with these arrangements in C-sharp. I'd say, 'It takes five hours more than necessary to learn this goddam thing. Don't write for some snobs, write for these guys here in the band.' But he was a beautiful arranger."

Mulligan, who was then 19, remembers the band as "the most professional band I'd ever written for. They were so professional they sometimes scared the hell out of me. They had no trouble playing anything I wrote."

"That band was challenging," agrees Gene. "I liked keeping up with these young sons of guns." The youngsters liked it, too. "For almost five years that band was really some-

Gene wears the uniform of the Westchester softball team he organized, in this 1970 picture. He and teammate Steven Raskinsky joke with Gene's adopted son (atop drum) and schoolmate.

thing," says Fagerquist. "It was a pleasure to go to work. Gene was a beautiful leader and a great, warm guy."

Everything was going smoothly. Gene remarried Ethel in 1947 and she stayed with him until her death in 1955. The band made such notable recordings as *Leave Us Leap* (with freeze beat), the flag-waving *Lover* and the Mulligan arrangements of *How High the Moon* and *Disc Jockey Jump*, which preserved its with-it sound. Gene even created a trio within the band; it was born at a recording session. "The session was going badly," says Gene, "all the guys were squabbling and starting to drive me crazy." So he sent everyone home but pianist Teddy Napoleon and saxophonist Charlie Ventura, who stayed to record an award-winning version of *Dark Eyes*.

Gene used the trio to alternate with the big band on one-nighters and give the sidemen some rest. "But they began abusing it," he says sadly. "A guy would get lost for an hour, and you'd find him across the street at the gas station—out on hard drugs. Deterioration set in. The feeling was gone. I lost some of the guys I didn't want to lose. So you got younger kids and they couldn't play the charts and on top of that they were junkies, too."

Krupa threatened to fire anybody he caught using drugs, "but I couldn't stay with them all the time" and in 1949 got some bad publicity when three of his men were booked for possession of marijuana. In 1951, after an appendicitis attack, Gene broke up his band for good, but before he could get out of the hospital Norman Granz was haunting the place, nagging Gene to join such stars as Ella Fitzgerald, Oscar Peterson, Flip Phillips, Illinois Jacquet and Lester Young in his Jazz at the Philharmonic concert series.

Until 1957 Gene spent half of each year roaming the world with JATP ("Some of the receptions we got overseas were like the greatest days of the band") and the other half playing dates with his trio—Teddy Napoleon and either Eddie Shu or Charlie Ventura. In 1954 he and Cozy Cole opened a drum school in New York, but Gene soon turned the whole thing over to Cozy. "I didn't have the patience for teaching." In 1956 he played himself in *The Benny Goodman Story*, one of "a couple of dozen" films in which he has appeared, and in 1959 saw himself portrayed by Sal Mineo in *The Gene Krupa Story*.

With the real Krupa on the sound track, Mineo, who claims to have been a Krupa fan since his 16th year, gave a fair portrayal of Krupa in action, but the rest of the picture reflects little of Gene's real story or of his gentle humor. "Still," says Gene, "I do get TV residuals on that and a couple of the other pictures like *Some Like It Hot* I made with the band over the years."

The same year *The Gene Krupa Story* was released Gene married Patricia Bowler, an attractive bookkeeper 25 years his junior. They adopted two children, Marygrace and Gene Michael. After leaving Jazz at the Philharmonic, Krupa worked mostly in New York with his trio until a heart attack in 1960 and then the onset of emphysema forced him out of full-time work. An enthusiastic smoker since the age of eight ("It's harder to quit than booze or grass"), Gene has reduced his consumption to two packs a day. "I'm such a homebody now," he says. "I spent so much time on the road. I used to look in the lighted windows of homes and yearn for the same way of life. Now I have it."

The life he has now is often lonely but never empty. His second marriage ended in divorce in 1968, but he still keeps in close touch with his two adopted children. Emphesyma and ruptured spinal discs have repeatedly laid him low, but between bouts he is up and around, practicing daily on his drums, taking an occasional gig (which is often cut short by illness), and making extraordinary efforts to show up at benefits arranged in his name. Though temporarily crippled by his ailing back, he showed up in an ambulance at a combined softball game and jazz concert he staged in 1970 to aid retarded children, climbed out painfully, spoke briefly and was whisked back to the hospital. He also teaches drumming to retarded children and lectures to teen-agers on the dangers of drug addiction.

Whenever possible he gets other musicians to come and play with him at his home. "There are some days," Gene said recently, "when you play and those drums feel right to you and you can't do anything wrong; everything fits. You sit there and you're happy all of a sudden, everything is beautiful. The difference between that and the times when nothing goes right must be the difference between heaven and hell. When I had to lie in bed after my heart attack in 1960, I wasn't so much concerned about dying as I was about being able to play a little bit again. I've never felt more like playing than I do right now."

—MICHELE WOOD

Thousands of fans will always remember Gene Krupa as he looked in 1937, during the Goodman band's engagement at New York's Hotel Pennsylvania—young and handsome, tossing his curly black hair, sweating, grunting for sheer joy, and pounding out the exuberant rhythms that were the epitome of the Swing Era.

The Men Who Made the Music:
John Kirby

Dean Shaffner is a New York television executive with a taste for swing. In 1937, when he was a Harvard senior, he and a couple of buddies drove the eight or so hours down from Cambridge just for the privilege of listening to some good music on Manhattan's Swing Street.

Swing Street was 52nd Street between Fifth and Sixth Avenues, a neighborhood of solid old brownstones, once the homes of solid old New York families. During Prohibition, the families moved out and the speakeasies moved in. The Street's first musicians came in along with bootleg booze; more of them came after Repeal when the speakeasies became nightclubs and the Street blossomed with neon names: the Three Deuces, the Yacht Club, the Famous Door, Kelly's Stable, Club 18, Jam Club, Jimmy Ryan's, the Spotlight, the Little Club, Club Samoa, Tony's, Leon & Eddie's, and the Onyx Club.

Shaffner and his friends got as far as the Onyx where John Kirby and his Sextet were playing. "We stayed all night," recalls Shaffner, "hearing the greatest little band, the greatest music I'd ever heard outside of Duke Ellington. We got as close to the band as we could and stayed there as long as we could. It was an absolutely genius collection of musicians. For a small band, they produced more musicianship and sheer brilliance than any group of musicians I had ever seen.

"I remember O'Neil Spencer when he got tired of sitting at his drums would sometimes get up and, without breaking a beat, start drumming on the backs of chairs or would walk around drumming on the ceiling—this was a very low ceiling and the band was on a platform up a couple of feet. And that Billy Kyle—such a unique, delightful piano style!

Sumptuously arrayed in white tails, the John Kirby Sextet gently swings a classic melody to entertain diners in the lavish Pump Room of Chicago's Ambassador East Hotel. Left to right are O'Neil Spencer, Charlie Shavers, Kirby, Buster Bailey, Russell Procope and Billy Kyle. The Sextet rose to fame during the five months it played at the Pump Room in the winter of 1939-40 and never lacked engagements until it began to dissolve two years later.

The rhythm section of Fletcher Henderson's great band included in 1933-34 Kirby (left), Horace Henderson, guitarist Bernard Addison, drummer Walter Johnson. John Kirby first joined the band in 1928 but failed to meet Fletcher's standards. He went back to playing with lesser bands, rejoined Henderson in 1930 and, as he later said, "got the reputation as the smoothest bass in town."

"Then, later in the summer of 1937, I was going back to Portland, Ore., where I had grown up and we stopped overnight in New York. Naturally I wanted to go back to hear this great little band, and they were just as great as they had been before. Since I thought I might be going back to the West Coast for the rest of my life, I thought I'd like to have a record of who they were and got a copy of the menu and asked each of them to autograph it, which they very pleasantly did and I'd give a lot if I still had that menu today."

Shaffner's glowing recollection of the Kirby sound is valid. After a few changes in the lineup of the band, that sound became the particular property of six superb musicians whose talents interlocked like the pieces of a Chinese puzzle. Few other small groups, not even some excellent combos Kirby led toward the end of his life, could duplicate the full sound of the Onyx outfit or the unobtrusive, steady, inventive support of John Kirby's stalwart string bass. The Sextet played together a little less than four years and made only about 65 record sides. During this short busy life, the Sextet set standards for small-group swing that few others have approached and none has surpassed. Kirby himself, along with such performers as Walter Page and Israel Crosby, raised the art of bass playing to a new plateau from which younger men like Jimmy Blanton, Oscar Pettiford, Charlie Mingus and Ray Brown were able to launch into still higher and more fanciful flights.

Kirby started with the handicaps of being black and an orphan. He got no musical training and very little other education. He was left-handed to boot, and who ever heard of a first-rate lefty bassman? Nobody knows for sure where or when he was born or who his parents were. He was found, as a newborn babe, abandoned on a Baltimore street on Dec. 31, 1908. He kept the date as his birthdate; it was about all he had for a start in life. A foundling home placed him with a couple named Fred and Dolly Kirby. Fred died when John was four; Dolly, when he was six. He probably had other foster parents, but nobody knows now who they were. During a visit to Baltimore some 31 years later, Kirby tried in vain to find a trace of any of them.

Kirby never talked much about his early years. About all his friends can remember from fragments of conversation is that he had odd jobs around town, began to learn to play a trombone and worked as a dishwasher, busboy and waiter in a Pennsylvania Railroad diner. One day in 1925 or 1926 he got off the train in New York City with a trombone in his hand and all his money—$6—in a "grouch bag," a small sack tied to a string around his neck. He slept that night in an abandoned Harlem distillery. When he woke up, the trombone was gone. As soon as he could scrape up the money, he replaced the trombone with a tuba, which, he later remarked, "was a tougher instrument to steal."

For the next three or four years Kirby lived like a lot of other hopeful young black musicians in New York. He played with Bill Brown and his Brownies at the Star Ballroom on 42nd Street, with pianist Charlie Skeets at the Bedford Ballroom in Brooklyn, and with John C. Smith's Society Band at Harlem's Alhambra Ballroom. Wellman Braud, the great string bass player, took a fancy to the slim and taciturn young man, with his light skin and green eyes and curly brown hair. Braud fed and clothed Kirby for a while and began teaching him to play the big fiddle.

Tender Tuba and Solid Strings

Kirby made other friends: trombonist Jimmy Harrison and saxophonist Coleman Hawkins, two of the stars of Fletcher Henderson's band. They talked Fletcher into hiring Kirby, but John was not yet ready for the high-powered Henderson band. After a few months Fletcher let him go and Kirby went to Bill Brown. He still read music imperfectly, and he had a few things to learn yet about the string bass. "I remember one time," says drummer Cozy Cole, "when Kirby and I messed up an audition because we couldn't read it." But Kirby kept broadening himself musically, partly with help from Pops Foster, the great New Orleans bassist, who had just come to New York. By the spring of 1930, Kirby was ready for Henderson. Aided again by Harrison and Hawkins, he got back into Fletcher's band, playing both string bass and tuba. "He played his big bass horn with the reeds, his playing was that sensitive," said trumpeter Charlie Shavers in an interview with Time-Life Records shortly before his death in 1971. "If he had been an educated man with the sensitivity he had, I don't know what he mighta been."

"He had a sound like smooth velvet," says bassist Beverly Peer, "and the vibrato was just right—very warm."

But jobs for tuba players, even those of Kirby's stature, were few. The tuba came to jazz from the Old New Orleans marching bands and was never as swingable a voice as the more agile and versatile string bass. It stayed in jazz as long as it did chiefly because early recording machinery could not pick up the sound of a string bass. As recording techniques improved, so did the market for string bassists, and Kirby, like most jazz tuba players, switched to strings. He was playing string bass by the time he made his first recordings with the Henderson band—*Chinatown my Chinatown* and *Somebody Loves Me*—in October 1930.

Between 1930 and early 1937, Kirby played at various times with the bands of Henderson, Chick Webb and Lucky Millinder, and all through this period he played in recording sessions with dozens of little combos. The Kirby hallmarks—

Maxine Sullivan had been Mrs. Kirby about a year when they visited the Rudy Vallee show (above) *in 1939. Maxine's* Loch Lomond *was sometimes requested more than 30 times in a night.*

sensitivity, clarity, adaptability, tone, precision—are stamped on some 400 recordings made in those years. Despite the limited ability of these early recordings to convey a sense of musical presence, Kirby's tone on them is resonant and full. Even with a big band like Henderson's, playing fortissimo and at breakneck speed, the Kirby presence is there—a strong guiding force and a beat that never fails.

"John had a wonderful technique," says Lawrence Lucie, who sat near him in Henderson's rhythm section for a while. "His tone was good and so was his bow work. He was one of the first I knew who did double-stops—that is, playing two notes at a time the same way you would on a violin."

"Bass players in that era did a lot of slapping—letting the strings hit the fingerboard—but Kirby's notes were always clear and distinct," says Peer. "Kirby held his bow and played the way they did in a symphony orchestra." And he was very quick, Peer adds, at shifting from plucking the strings of his bass to bowing them.

"He was one of the best," says Cozy Cole. "You didn't play in Fletcher Henderson's band unless you were tops. Kirby used to study and practice all the time. He had good teachers,

And on Bass, John Kirby

During the 1930s, John Kirby played, mostly on record dates, with a stupendous array of great jazz musicians, some of whom are shown on these pages. Many of the 400-odd sides which Kirby took part in making during this period have become jazz classics.

 ## Trumpeters

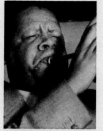  

Henry ("Red") Allen   **Bobby Stark**   **Harry James**

Taft Jordan   **Rex Stewart**   **Max Kaminsky**   **Jonah Jones**

Cootie Williams   **Roy Eldridge**   **Frankie Newton**   **Wingy Manone**

 ## Trombonists

Lawrence Brown   **Jimmy Harrison**   **Jack Teagarden**   **J. C. Higginbotham**

Floyd O'Brien   **Bennie Morton**   **Dicky Wells**   **Sandy Williams**

Drummers

Cozy Cole

Big Sid Catlett

Guitarist

Eddie Condon

Buddy Schutz

Pianists

Fletcher Henderson   **Lil Armstrong**

Claude Thornhill   **James P. Johnson**

Teddy Wilson   **Horace Henderson**

44

Gene Krupa

Chick Webb

Buddy Rich

Jo Jones

Saxophonists

Benny Carter

Charlie Barnet

Babe Russin

Hilton Jefferson

Chu Berry

Herschel Evans

Coleman Hawkins

Harry Carney

Ben Webster

Johnny Hodges

Bud Freeman

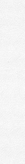

Jess Stacy

Willie ("The Lion") Smith

Clarinetists

Benny Goodman

Artie Shaw

Edmond Hall

Albert Nicholas

Johnny Dodds

Vocalists

Jelly Roll Morton

Midge Williams

Billie Holiday

Mildred Bailey

Ethel Waters

but he never had any formal music training like at a music school. He had a great tone and great precision in his playing. You could hear every note. He had God-given talent. He was very flexible. He could play the bass in any style. Bass players idolized him."

Kirby's bowing in the slower recordings sounds somber and intent, which was the way the man himself impressed most people. "Sometimes we would come on a date," says guitarist Jimmy McLin, "and he might not even speak. That was his natural way. A lot of people didn't like him for that. I didn't understand him, but after we were thrown together so much I just recognized it as his way."

But Kirby could talk easily enough about what really interested him, Lawrence Lucie remembers. "You'd never really know what he was thinking," says Lucie, "until he got you off to one side—only then would he start talking. He always wanted to talk music and his own ideas of creating something new in music." Lucie remembers Kirby as "very ambitious" and unwilling to be "just another player in a big band."

The moody young Kirby went on playing in the background, thoughtfully observing the way the talented British composer-arranger Reginald Foresythe combined Kirby's string bass with two clarinets (Benny Goodman was one of them), a bassoon, a tenor, two alto saxes and drums (Gene Krupa), or the way Teddy Wilson used trumpet, clarinet, saxophone, piano, guitar, drums and string bass—very close to the lineup Kirby himself eventually adopted.

The names of the jazzmen who made recordings with John Kirby in the '30s form a brilliant array—a sort of rainbow of the art form (see pp. 44-45). He was much in demand for backing such vocalists as Mildred Bailey, Billie Holiday and Maxine Sullivan—his bass was like a voice that sang along with theirs.

At these sessions Kirby would get to know how a musician played, says McLin. "He'd do a record with him or maybe jam with him and not say anything. But later he might offer him a job." Kirby was not only picking out future sidemen as he listened and played but was gaining a remarkable depth of experience in the hundred and one ways a small group can play together and in the effects of shifts in personnel, in arrangers and in the voicings of instruments. By 1937 Kirby was more than ready to lead a group of his own.

He got his chance because Joe Helbock, owner of the Onyx Club, needed a new house band. The jazz-loving Helbock had been the favorite bootlegger of a lot of musicians; his clientele included Paul Whiteman and the Dorsey brothers. The next step up for a prosperous bootlegger was to have his own speakeasy; in 1930 Helbock opened one in an old brownstone at 35 West 52nd Street, within easy walking distance of both the NBC (Fifth Avenue at 55th) and CBS (Madison and 52nd) studios. Musicians flocked to the place,

At the Onyx Club the muted trumpet of Charlie Shavers blends with Kirby's bass. Shavers, the band's youngest member, learned much from his colleagues, became the Sextet's chief arranger and with his wry humor effectively molded its musical personality.

walking down a couple of steps to the entry ("What they called in them days an English basement," says Joe) and then climbing a flight of stairs. "You pushed a button," says Joe, "and there was a door with a slot in it and you said, 'I'm from Local 802,' and you were in."

Refreshments at the Onyx were much like those at the Street's other speakeasies. As the late Charles Edward Smith once wrote in a loving chronicle of Swing Street: "At some there was vintage Scotch, brought down the Island (Long Island) from ship rendezvous off Montauk Point by drivers of fast trucks with rolls of bills for payoffs and guns for hijackers. At others there was whiskey blended in the Bronx, beer from Hoboken and 'London' gin made on the premises."

Inside, the Onyx Club was painted in black, dark blue and silver. "That's how come I called it the Onyx Club," says Joe. "Those are the colors of onyx, someone told me—black and silver."

Wilder Hobson, a pioneer American jazz historian, has described the scene at the Onyx Club: "There was a shadowy hall and a couple of drinking rooms, the rear room containing a bar, one of those push-ball games, a shabby upright piano, a few tables and some wicker chairs. Along about five in the afternoon, Joe Sullivan or Charley Bourne or Art Tatum would be playing the piano, but it was all so casual that if you hadn't known they were engaged by the management you might have supposed they had just dropped in and sat down. This effect was heightened by the fact that any of the guests could make music if he wished."

Club Within the Club

Many guests did make music and also used the Onyx as a place to drink, stash their instruments and make phone calls between radio shows and recording dates. The Five Spirits of Rhythm became the first house band, with Teddy Bunn on guitar, Virgil Scroggins drumming with two whisk brooms on a suitcase covered with wrapping paper, and the other three playing ukulele-like instruments called tipples. One of the tipple players, Leo Watson, also did scat singing and in time became a featured vocalist with Artie Shaw and Gene Krupa. He also became a dedicated if unorthodox drummer and once launched into a solo that went on for more than an hour. The customers at the nightclub where he was playing began to complain, but all efforts by the management failed to silence him. As two cops finally dragged Leo away, he was still steadily beating a side drum clutched under one arm.

Through Prohibition and into Repeal, musicians followed the Onyx as Helbock moved from Number 35 to 72 West 52nd and finally to 62. At Number 72, the decor included huge portraits, nearly six feet high, of musical figures like Paul Whiteman, Mildred Bailey and the Dorseys. "Some fella painted them," says Joe. "Not that I asked; he wanted to. It didn't cost me anything."

One day in 1935 a fire of mysterious origin gutted Number 72. "All I know is that my partner collected the insurance and got lost," says Joe. Helbock rebuilt the Onyx with money from friends and reopened with a band that included trombonist Mike Riley and cornetist Eddie Farley. This duo made such a hit with the Swing Era anthem, *The Music Goes 'Round and Around,* that the Onyx was jammed for months. The next year, 1936, Helbock staged New York's first "swing music concert" which, among other things, helped to launch the little-known Artie Shaw as a bandleader.

Another star of that concert was Hezekiah ("Stuff") Smith, the hot violinist, whose sextet Helbock had brought in from Buffalo to replace the Riley-Farley outfit as the Onyx house band. In 1937 Stuff was lured to Hollywood by an offer to appear in a movie. The deal fell through, but by that time Helbock had replaced him at the Onyx with Kirby and a band that included Teddy Bunn and Leo Watson from the Spirits of Rhythm, along with Frankie Newton, a big-toned trumpeter; Pete Brown, a fat and engaging alto saxophonist; pianist Don Frye; and one of the most limpid and exciting of clarinetists, Buster Bailey.

This was just about the instrumentation Kirby wanted, and with it he established a style that comes through clearly in one of the records he made in August 1937 with Newton, Bailey and Brown, Babe Russin on tenor sax, O'Neil Spencer on drums and Claude Thornhill, a rising young freelance arranger and pianist, on piano. The vocalist was a pretty young thing from Pittsburgh who had been discovered by Gladys Mosier, the pianist in Ina Ray Hutton's all-girl band and who had started singing at the Onyx Club about the time Kirby opened there.

Thornhill was helping the girl launch her career. He advised her to change her name from Marietta Williams to Maxine Sullivan and wrote an arrangement of *Loch Lomond* for her. Thornhill's sprightly piano and Maxine's clear, soft young voice helped to make the number a hit on records and at the Onyx. Kirby's solid bass helped, too, though he didn't get his name on the record label.

Compatibility of Talents

But in the classic American tradition, he got the girl. He and Maxine were married in 1938. By that time Buster Bailey was the only sideman from the original group who was still with Kirby. The others Kirby replaced with musicians whose talents more closely fitted the sextet style he was developing. He had picked up pianist Billy Kyle, drummer Spencer and trumpeter Charlie Shavers from the disintegrating Lucky Millinder Blue Rhythm Band, which Kirby himself had left early in 1937. Russell Procope, whom Kirby remembered from the Fletcher Henderson band, returned from a European tour in time to become the final member.

"I was downtown one night," Procope recalls, "and I think I'd been to Madison Square Garden—the old site on Eighth Avenue—where a young man by the name of Joe Louis had just annihilated some other young man, and I was walking along 52nd Street. I went down and heard John Kirby's band and he asked me to come up and play something with him. It seems that he liked what he heard me play."

Kirby's five sidemen offered a remarkable diversity of skills. Bailey was a clarinetist of such polish that he could—and did—sit in with symphony orchestras. Kyle's light touch

on the piano and the dancing rhythms of Spencer's drums perfectly complemented the fluid lines of Procope's alto sax and the penetrating punctuations of Shavers' muted trumpet. They combined with Kirby to plait six different styles into one consistent sound.

The marvelous compatibility of these six talents quickly made the group outstanding even on Swing Street where, both during and after hours, practically all the great names in swing were either playing gigs or sitting in with each other. Only Swing Street, with its elbow-to-elbow clubs could have held them all. At night the whole Street surged with people going from place to place to play or to listen.

A lot of the musicians flowed into the White Rose Bar on Sixth Avenue just off 52nd, where drinks were cheaper than in the clubs and a delicious free lunch was always available. Russell Procope remembers it as a place where musicians could slap down a $5 bill, saying, "Keep it coming till that's gone," and then concentrate on conversation and Scotch (35¢ a straight shot), confident that any change they had coming would be put into their pockets before they toddled away.

On leaving the White Rose after a few intermission drinks, musicians sometimes stumbled into the wrong club and played the next set with somebody else's band—no great wonder since the clubs were not only close-set but often changed their names and marquees. Thus one club might find itself suddenly bandless, while its neighbor's bandstand was overflowing, but not for long. "Owners of clubs would just hire three musicians," says Cozy Cole, "because they knew that before the night was over they would have one or two others sitting in. The union finally put a stop to this."

A musician like Coleman Hawkins, say, or Benny Carter could—and did—start the evening at the Street's western border, near Sixth Avenue, and play his way east to Fifth Avenue, being greeted like good news from home at every club where he chose to sit in. Goggle-eyed patrons heard some of the world's greatest swing musicians in impromptu combinations that might include sections of five trumpets or five saxes. Competitions inevitably arose. "The cutting sessions there were just fantastic," says pianist Billy Taylor.

On Sunday afternoons there were jam sessions, which

Soon after marrying Maxine Sullivan, Kirby proudly examines the sheet music for a song he and Maxine had just recorded. With him on the bandstand of the Onyx Club are (left to right) Procope, Kyle, an unidentified visitor, Bailey, Shavers, Spencer.

were really free-form jazz concerts, up and down the Street. Musicians were free to sit in, the public to come and listen. "You moved from the Famous Door to the Hickory House," says Helen Oakley Dance who then wrote for the French magazine, *Le Jazz Hot*. "You heard great music, had a couple of drinks, saw everyone you knew. It was a very groovy scene."

A couple of hundred lucky people crowded into the upstairs room at the Famous Door on one of these Sunday afternoons and heard Bessie Smith, Empress of the Blues, sing a few of her famous numbers, accompanied by Bunny Berigan, his mighty trumpet whispering behind her with unaccustomed softness.

In an era famous for small-group swing, the Kirby band stood out among all the Swing Street bands, the recording studio combos, the little bands of men like Raymond Scott and Teddy Wilson, and the subdivisions of the big bands, like the Benny Goodman trios, quartets and sextets, Chick Webb and his Little Chicks, Bob Crosby's Bob Cats, Tommy Dorsey's Clambake Seven, Artie Shaw's Gramercy Five and Woody Herman's Woodchoppers.

Many of these small bands had interesting instrumentations and gifted performers and arrangers. None had the Kirby combination of fine, well-matched musicians who were both personally and musically compatible, who played and rehearsed together extensively, and who loved their work.

Every man in the Sextet was at or near the top among practitioners of his instrument and each was an impeccable soloist, but their skills showed to greatest advantage in what Charlie Shavers called their "blend of mentalities."

"They played as though everyone had a piece of the action," says Maxine Sullivan. Vic Schoen, who was house arranger for Decca in those days, agrees: "The ideas, the inclinations, everything came together. The chemistry was just right."

"They melted together nice, real nice," says Jimmy McLin. "It was an original, good sound. You could hear everything going on. John was very essential to that sound. His bass filled in behind every soloist and spread around over it. He had an outstanding knack for blending that bass."

Everything they played fitted their style because they chose their arrangements carefully. The group itself produced most of them. "We sit like one big family around the table," Kirby once said. "The piano tries it, and then the clarinet and the trumpet. We decide who's going to carry the melody or maybe the melody switches. Then we just kind of work it around until we get a blending effect, and the arranger writes it down."

Shavers and Kyle did most of the writing down. Charlie's particular sparkle shines through on his arrangements of *Front and Center* and *Blues Petite*, his lighthearted rechore-

Kirby and Gene Krupa appeared at Carnegie Hall in 1942 with guitarist Eddie Condon, saxophonist Bud Freeman, clarinetist Pee Wee Russell and trumpeter Max Kaminsky. They provided the finale for a piano and organ recital by Fats Waller, who stunned an audience that had been expecting jazz with a program that included variations on a theme by Tchaikowsky.

ographing of Grieg's *Anitra's Dance* and his own composition, *Undecided*. Billy arranged the pop tunes, and to help with arrangements of classical compositions Kirby sometimes brought in outside talent like arranger Lou Singer, a Juilliard graduate.

Kirby's system of using only top instrumentalists and encouraging all of them to contribute ideas reminds Lawrence Lucie of Duke Ellington: "You had star musicians making up things in their head and putting these things together and keeping them set. That was Duke's idea, too—he had a different style, of course, but the same concept of jazz organization."

It took a lot of good ideas to get the Kirby sound out of six instruments. "There was clarinet, alto sax and trumpet— all high-pitched instruments," says Maxine Sullivan. "To voice these instruments to get top and bottom called for writing for the instruments and using the full range of all the horns to get a full ensemble sound. They would rehearse the ensemble parts, and the solos would have to fit in with the flavor of what they were playing. It required a terrific amount of technical work and virtuosity."

The Kirby musicians memorized so many of their arrangements that some people thought they couldn't read. In fact, they all learned to read one way or another. Charlie Shavers, who joined the band as a kid of 20, learned from the older men like Procope and Bailey. Kirby, like Shavers, had had

to learn music on the job but, as Vic Schoen says, "He put 20 years of work into ten; that's how he compensated."

The band's remarkable evenness of talent, unanimity of taste and style, and the effects of constant rehearsals showed at its first recording session. The Sextet ripped off *Undecided, From A Flat to C, Rehearsin' for a Nervous Breakdown* and *Pastel Blue* without a second try on any of them—an almost unheard-of display of perfection.

"We recorded at Decca on 57th Street," Shavers said, "where they had that wooden Indian with the sign saying, 'Don't forget the melody.' The first time we played a record date we had our scene down so straight we did four sides in four takes. That was a wild thing. The A. and R. man came by and said, 'What time is it? What the hell is this?' But we couldn't have played them better."

They recorded as "John Kirby and His Onyx Club Boys" because the club was more famous than Kirby. For all his standing among musicians, he had no national following yet and had run a poor third among bassists in a 1937 *Down Beat* poll. The Sextet was lucky that its fortunes did not depend on Kirby's personal flamboyance.

"He'd go buy a suit," says Procope, "and we'd be waiting for him to show a little flash, and when he'd come back, he'd look exactly as he had before. He wouldn't even put on a red tie. We used to call him 'the insurance man' because that's exactly what he looked like."

The insurance man smoked a lot—but only tobacco. He liked a drink but never seemed to get drunk. On or off the stand he was solid, substantial, quiet, dryly witty and little given to solos—musical or conversational. But getting to know him well was rewarding. "He was warm, rich," says Vic Schoen, "like an old wine. He was so bright and quick. He was totally attractive."

"He hung out with his men all the time," remembers saxophonist Budd Johnson. "He was never a put-on or anything like that."

"Kirby was a doll," said Shavers. "Kirby would give you the shirt off his back." Procope remembers that when Kirby hired him "he was going to pay me something like $60 or $70 a week, but before I could start he called me at home and said, 'Listen, about that amount of money we talked about; that doesn't seem right to me—let's raise it another $10.'"

Kirby did show a little flash when it came to cars. He liked them big and fast. Trombonist Sandy Williams says Kirby was copying his friend Coleman Hawkins in this. "John always tried to act like Hawk, who was a couple of years older," says Sandy, "and because Hawk liked automobiles, he'd always follow him on the highway."

"Kirby had a La Salle," says Cozy Cole. "He talked me into getting a La Salle. It was a big, fancy car. Kirby loved to drive fast. He was traveling around with Fletcher doing a lot of one-night stands, and he would make what was a three-hour drive for somebody else in an hour and a half. He just loved fast cars."

Through 1938 and much of 1939 the band drew to the Onyx nightly crowds of devoted listeners like Dean Shaffner and his friends. Its 25 record sides did moderately well. But the Sextet remained little known outside New York until it happened to blow some soft notes at the right minute.

"We used to blow loud and raucous," said Charlie Shavers. "Maybe it started getting on my nerves, so one day I sat down and made a last chorus of *Rose Room* of exaggerated softness, just to see how soft we could play. The guy from the Pump Room in Chicago came in, Ernie Byfield. We were playin' *Rose Room*. If he had walked in five minutes earlier we'd have blown him out the door. But we were playing the only soft thing we had and after that we came off. He hired us on the spot for three weeks."

The Pump Room and Beyond

The Pump Room in Chicago's Ambassador East Hotel was a lavish namesake of the rather austere Pump Room in Bath, England, where Beau Nash had set the tone of 18th century society. A portrait of the Beau himself, said to have been found in a New York junk shop, hung above the ample bar. The spacious Pump Room's walls and its glassware were deep blue. Its booths and banquettes were upholstered in white leather. Light from crystal sconces and chandeliers glittered on little black "coffee boys" costumed, from 18th century prints, in plumed white satin turbans and emerald satin jackets. Waiters in scarlet jackets and knee breeches served skewered meats and crêpes suzette gloriously aflame.

Byfield had originally hired a small rumba band but felt it didn't quite measure up to the Pump Room's elegance. Kirby's music seemed more appropriate and so did Kirby's men after Byfield had outfitted them in all-white full evening dress. Kirby quickly toned down the Sextet's sound to accommodate the Pump Room's decorous diners. *Down Beat* reporter Ted Toll found the Sextet swinging lightly through adaptations of Grieg, Chopin, Schubert, Debussy, Dvořák and other classics, as well as the numbers the band had previously recorded and some new ones the band had worked up since coming to Chicago—*Twentieth Century Closet, Opus 5, Jumpin' in the Pump Room, Blues Petite* and *Milumbu.*

"It was really classical jazz," says Budd Johnson. "It wasn't a big sound—more subdued. That was one of the main points that made the band so well-loved—people could eat and carry on a conversation while the band was playing. They could hear themselves talk."

Toll reported that the Kirby band included some of "the very finest jazz musicians in the world" playing with "agility, taste and perfection." He continued: "No tempo seems too much for them, no rhythms too intricate, no pianissimo too soft (and that's truly an accomplishment for a jazz band). The Kirby band merits a lot more promotion and attention than its handlers have been giving it."

Wow! The Sextet stayed more than five months at the Pump Room and after that was booked practically solid for the rest of its life. The Music Corporation of America, biggest bookers in the business, kept the band so busy in and around New York that it seldom went anywhere else. The Sextet became the first black band to play the Waldorf-Astoria, appeared on a CBS network radio show, Flow Gently, Sweet

Rhythm, with commentary by actor Canada Lee, and then, on Duffy's Tavern, became the first black band to appear on a nationally sponsored major network radio series.

As Kirby's fame grew, his marriage to Maxine Sullivan crumbled. She had appeared with the band at the Onyx Club and toured with it later, but *Loch Lomond* had made her even more famous than Kirby. She was a star and, like most stars, had an urge to shine on-her own. Not long after Gene Krupa left Benny Goodman, Maxine left the Sextet and went out as a single. Success pushed her and Kirby apart. They were divorced in 1941. Kirby soon remarried. He was never alone for long.

"I haven't the faintest idea how he did it," says Russell Procope, "but women would always give him everything. There were always women who wanted to take care of him." He'd get up there on the stand in his insurance man suit, Procope says, and women in the audience would sit up. "He did attract attention," Shavers remembered. "If I told you some names you'd be surprised, and I mean movie stars."

Kirby's stunning second wife Margaret, now married to retired baseball umpire Emmett Ashford, knows what *she* saw in Kirby. "He was a beautiful man, so sweet," she says. "Kirby had the physique of a man who could wear clothes beautifully. And he wore the best. Physically, he reminded me of Beethoven. He had that face. I had Beethoven's death mask over the Capehart, lit indirectly. People would come in and they would gasp, 'Why, it looks just like Kirby!' "

Mrs. Ashford recalls idyllic evenings in their 126th Street apartment with the Sextet and friends like Coleman Hawkins

Kirby seemed moody and taciturn to many but could relax amiably with musicians like Edgar Sampson (left) whom he liked and respected. They first met in Henderson's band and were playing with Chick Webb in 1935, the date of this picture. Sampson played sax and violin, wrote many jazz standards and arranged for big-name bands like Benny Goodman's and Artie Shaw's.

and Art Tatum sitting around the Capehart under the Beethoven death mask listening to classical music, some of which inspired Kirby arrangements. "The Sextet itself was such a close-knit family," says Margaret. "They would discuss things and out would come Schubert's *Serenade.*"

They were a happy family. Raymond Scott's six-man "Quintet," which blossomed about the same time as Kirby's group and which Shavers called "our only competition," achieved a distinctive and engaging sound from almost the same instruments Kirby used and by some of the same methods. Like Kirby, Scott combined the ideas of his sidemen, but he dominated the whole process and his men loathed the mechanical perfection they felt he demanded. With Kirby's men, Vic Schoen remembers, a recording session was a blast. "It was difficult to create in a recording studio the atmosphere that most jazz musicians need," he says, "but they would play together for a while and pretty soon the atmosphere was all emotional . . . just right."

"We'd be goin' down the road at 80 miles an hour singin' *Row, Row, Row Your Boat* in harmony," Shavers said. "It was that kind of band. They used to treat me like a kid, like they were uncles. 'Where you goin'?' 'Do you know what *time* it is?' " For the pleasures of playing with Kirby, Shavers and Procope turned down offers from leaders like Duke Ellington and Tommy Dorsey.

The band was immensely popular on many levels. Mrs. Ashford remembers its appeal to the "carriage trade" and how "Tyrone Power would sweep into Cafe Society Uptown when Kirby and the group were playing there.

"Kirby and Cab Calloway were playing that big jazz hall in Chicago one time, and Cab was on first. He was sensational with his big 16-piece band. And then Kirby came on, just the six of them. He had that crowd eating out of their palms. Cab said to Kirby that he was going to fire his whole band if that was what Kirby could do with just six musicians."

"Man, we really caught on," says Procope with a reminiscent sigh. "By the time I was drafted, we were playing at clubs all over Manhattan. We were so much in demand that we couldn't even cross the river to go into Jersey. Sometimes we'd be playing in one place, and during the intermission we'd all dash off in a car owned by a disc jockey to play somewhere else. We'd play three or four numbers—until our intermission was due to be up—then we'd dash back."

When the group recorded *Beside the River Clyde* and *How Do I Know It's Real?* with Maxine Sullivan, on March 19, 1942, it sounded as great as ever, but soon after, suddenly and sadly, the Sextet began to fall apart. Drummer O'Neil Spencer went first. Kirby had laid him off for a while and then brought him back to the band, but it soon became evident that Spencer was losing his mind. "He was always a little strange," Margaret Ashford recalls. "He would sit up there on the stage knitting—blankets and baby clothes." Then on a night in 1942, the band finished a set and Spencer kept on playing.

"Now, Spencer, stop it," said Kirby.

"Don't you see all those people looking at me?" asked Spencer.

Kirby had to let Spencer go for good; he died of tuberculosis in 1944. By then, Kyle and Procope were gone, too. When Kyle was drafted, says Mrs. Ashford, "Kirby started cracking up. He became more and more flagrant with his women. He wasn't keeping his appointments. Then Russell Procope was drafted. Kirby was beside himself. Trummy Young would sit in, other greats would sit in, but that unity wasn't there any more."

A Vanished Shimmer

Shavers remembered that after Procope left, "we put in Benny Carter, and you know you can't get around Benny Carter." Most musicians would agree Carter is unbeatable on alto sax. "But it didn't sound the same," Charlie sadly recalled. The new men in the Sextet were looser, harder-swinging but less disciplined players. The music lost its light, airy shimmer; it sounded good but it sounded like a lot of other groups.

The changes were too much for Shavers, who left in 1944 to play first for Raymond Scott and then for Tommy Dorsey. "The Kirby band had broken up," Charlie mourned, "and that was my heart, my baby."

"I think Kirby thought the record would turn forever, that it would go on and on, and he would always be its Pied Piper," says Mrs. Ashford. "When the Sextet fell apart, what family he had, there wasn't anything else. Kirby went into his shell. He wasn't a learned man. He didn't finish school. Losing his band just about stabbed him. He tried to make comebacks. In those days the demand was kaput. Bookings became less and less. His contacts became less and less. He just sort of went along with the tide. He didn't even grab at straws. His pride wouldn't let him take a job with a band. He'd been a leader for too long."

Kirby was drinking heavily in spite of a doctor's warning that he had diabetes and should lay off booze. He was also told to avoid fish because of an allergy. His wife left him. Even his familiar environment was crumbling. Burlesque shows, prostitutes and dope pushers were creeping into Swing Street. Kirby made his last recording in 1946 and the Sextet's story seemed ended. But it had one final flourish. In December 1950 Kirby appeared at a Carnegie Hall concert with all the living members of the Sextet, and Big Sid Catlett on drums. The concert as a whole was a flop, but the Sextet sparkled. "The actual Kirby moments were a musical as well as a nostalgic delight," *Down Beat* reported. "Charlie Shavers, despite a spot too much clowning, was in magnificent form; Buster Bailey still held those legitimate long notes prettily for *Dawn on the Desert;* Russell Procope played cool, clean alto and Billy Kyle his humorous, happy piano."

Nothing was ever the same for Kirby after his Sextet began to break up in 1942. He formed other groups and for a while toured the Midwest with various outfits like the one in this picture, taken in the late '40s, probably in a Milwaukee bar. Left to right are Freddie Radcliffe, Kirby, Benny Rhodes, Roy Grant and Pee Wee Jackson. But the famous Sextet sound was gone. Kirby moved to California and was planning a new start when he died in 1952.

The sidemen went back to their various bands and Kirby took to playing gigs in uptown bars. Jimmy McLin remembers playing with Kirby in his last job in New York "in a little joint in Harlem called the West Indian George, at 137th and Lenox. Just bass and guitar. He could drink a pretty good drink by then—Scotch and soda. He tried to get me to go with him to California."

McLin refused, a decision that still distresses him. "But I guess he would have died even if I had gone along," he says sadly. Charlie Shavers, who had a West Coast job lined up, agreed to drive to California with Kirby in John's big, black Cadillac. He was anxious to get Kirby out of New York. "He wasn't workin'," Charlie said, "and I didn't want people—as big as he had been—lookin' at him like he was nothing. We drove to California. He got a little foothold goin'. People out there were more tolerant."

With help from friends like Shavers and Benny Carter, Kirby got a few jobs. He shared a rented pad on Harvard Boulevard in Los Angeles with a congenial lady named Mary and even stopped drinking. Russell Procope came through and spent a couple of days with Kirby. "He was full of plans,"

Procope remembers. "He was talking about getting things going again."

Three weeks after Procope's visit, on June 14, 1952, a neighbor came running to tell Shavers that Kirby seemed to be in a coma. "I went over and he was dead," Shavers said. "This cat ate a can of sardines. I saw the can. He came back in and keeled over."

Benny Carter came over. So did Kirby's wife, who had been about to divorce him. "It was real poverty," she says of Kirby's last home. "Their end tables were packing crates. Kirby had always had a three-carat diamond ring that was security for him. Even that was gone. He didn't have anything to be buried in. Benny took care of everything, paid for the funeral, the headstone."

For his final appearance, John Kirby had about him the things he had loved most—music, friends and beautiful women. "Considering Kirby had been out of touch for so long, it was a beautiful funeral," says Mrs. Ashford. "It was nicely attended. There were flowers and telegrams from all over. Mary rode in the family car. I thought that was right."

—FREDERIC RAMSEY JR., AND THE EDITORS

The Music in This Volume

By all rights, swing should have blown taps for itself in the late 1940s and been carried off to join ragtime and the one-step in the Valhalla of popular music. After the disheartening weeks in 1946 when half a dozen of the biggest bands in the business broke up, there seemed to be no future for it. Many of the leaders reformed their bands and played bravely on. But it wasn't the same. New idols and new kinds of jazz were pushing into the spotlight. Hurt by the competition of TV, theaters no longer could afford to hire bands. Hotels that once broadcast their ballroom music on coast-to-coast radio networks now found that radio had been increasingly usurped by disc jockeys who did not need live bands. Ballrooms found that people just didn't dance so much any more—at least not to jazz. And musicians, mustered out of service, found it hard to get jobs. Their plight was summed up by an ad in an Atlantic City paper that read: "WANTED Piano Player who can open oysters and clams."

In a way, the competition for jobs helped swing, for leaders had their pick of sidemen and the bands recovered a quality lost during the war. Cautiously at first but then more eagerly, they fitted the harmonies and rhythms of the new jazz into their music and kept swing from becoming merely an echo of itself. Old hands found themselves playing less wildly but with more precision and polish. The swing of the decades after the war has a refreshing variety of styles, and much of it has a beautiful sheen and fullness. When rock came, of course, jazz was no longer in the running as mass music. Swing settled into place as one of the many forms—bop, cool, modern, progressive—that jazz developed. It wasn't king any more. But it was—and still is—swing.

SIDE ONE

Band 1 THE KID FROM RED BANK
Count Basie version

The kid, who became the Count, was born in Red Bank, N.J., and this number was written to celebrate that fact. It also celebrates Basie's instrument, the piano, which can hardly wait for the brass to open *The Kid from Red Bank* before making itself heard. It ripples into its first chorus, stressing a cluster of treble notes. It waits for the band to echo the theme, comes back in a striding passage that moves into another note cluster, and still another. Running up and down, putting in a little ragtime, it moves nimbly over the ever-present bass, engaging the band in a little dialogue, skittering through some scales, hammering at a single note. It never lets the band really catch up and, at the end, caps the band's down-the-scale passage with an up-the-scale passage of its own.

William Basie had his first piano lessons in Red Bank, from his mother and, he recalls, from a "wonderful German lady named Holloway." His important musical education began in Harlem when, as a teen-ager, he met a jazz genius only a few months older than himself—by name, Thomas ("Fats") Waller. From Fats, Basie absorbed the styles that Waller, in turn, had learned from the great James P. Johnson and Willie ("The Lion") Smith. Little tributes to Waller can be heard throughout *The Kid from Red Bank* in the striding passages and the ragtime touches.

Red Bank lost Basie for good when he went west with a show and was stranded in Kansas City, Mo., which turned out to be one of the happiest misfortunes in jazz. For there Basie latched onto the ebullient Kansas City style of jazz, got his first chance to lead a band, gained the title of "Count" and was on his way to fame. But his home town remembers the kid proudly, and on its jubilee Red Bank gave him a banquet and proposed—although the proposal has not yet been adopted—renaming one of its busiest avenues "Basie Street."

Band 2 SATIN DOLL
Duke Ellington version

When the Duke turns on the elegance, nobody in swing can match him for sophisticated polish—and in *Satin Doll*, with its good-humored self-assurance and worldly air, the Duke outdid himself.

The piano (the Duke originally, of course) brings on the doll with a chiming figure that is answered by the bass. As the saxes play the melody, the trombones move up a scale that ends in a lovely counter-melody. The tenor sax pushes in briefly; the brass flares. After an interlude, the bass and a single piano note lead the saxes and muted trumpets into the last part of the chorus, the trombones uttering low rasps. The trumpet (Ray Nance originally) takes a bright-toned chorus, inflecting the way Bunny Berigan used to. Then the band, having walked the doll around, comes back to where it started.

Duke Ellington is known to be a romantic man, and people have wondered whom he had in mind when he wrote *Satin Doll*. Mercer Ellington, his son, responded to that question when Stanley Dance, author of *The World of Duke Ellington*, asked it: "*Satin Doll* was probably a matter of Ellington sitting at the piano, comping or fooling around, and hearing something. Sometimes when he's accompanying a soloist, he plays a figure that has a complete identification of its own, and he'll either note it mentally or jot it down and come back and make a song of it. Some of the questions most often asked him are: 'Who is *Satin Doll*? Who is *Sophisticated Lady*?' I think at the time those numbers were written he didn't visualize any one woman. That is my opinion. *Satin Doll* is for everybody who happens to be with a wonderful lady that night."

Band 3 SWANEE RIVER BOOGIE
Commanders version

There is considerable—and understandable—confusion about the band called the Commanders. First and still best-remembered were Irving Aaronson's Commanders of the '20s and '30s, whose soft-spoken leader had an eye for talent that led him to hire, when they were still fledglings, such future stars as Artie Shaw, Claude Thornhill and Gene Krupa. In 1953 arranger Tutti Camarata used the name for a group that came together to make some recordings. Later, Eddie Grady, the drummer, took some of the personnel out on tour. Then trombonist Warren Covington took over the name and the group for a couple of years.

Swanee River Boogie was done by Camarata's bunch, an all-star collection whose roster can be found on page 63. "We called ourselves the Commanders," explains Camarata, "to convey the notion of not having a leader. The lineup was unconventional—only two saxes but four trombones." *Swanee River Boogie* doesn't take boogie too seriously, giving it an offhand, shuffle-rhythm treatment. The piano has some nice harmonies and some player-piano octave trills. The trumpet is straight jazz, and the trombones display a kind of rough togetherness as they dominate the last chorus with their out-of-breath effects.

If the idea of putting a boogie beat to the hallowed Swanee River upsets you, just think of the name as Pedee River. That's what it was in Stephen Foster's song originally—"Way down upon de Pedee Ribber" was what Foster wrote in his manuscript. His brother Morrison told how it was changed. One day Stephen came in and asked him: "What is a good name of two syllables for a Southern river?" Morrison's first suggestion, Yazoo, wouldn't do. Pedee was ruled out. "I then took down an atlas," recounted Morrison, "and opened the map of the United States. My finger stopped at the Swanee [Suwannee], a little river in Florida emptying into the Gulf of Mexico. 'That's it exactly,' exclaimed he, delighted." And in Foster's manuscript of *Old Folks at Home*, "Pedee" is crossed out and over it is written "Swanee."

Band 4 JUST A-SITTIN' AND A-ROCKIN'
Stan Kenton version

The rocking chair has a popular but pathetic place in jazz. Hoagy Carmichael's *Rockin' Chair* ("Old Rockin' Chair's got me, Cane by my side, Fetch me that gin, son, 'fore I tan your hide . . .") is a lament for lost youth. The Duke Ellington-Billy Strayhorn *Just A-Sittin' and A-Rockin'* is a lament for lost love, written in the same vein—and at about the same time—as the Duke's *Don't Get Around Much Anymore* (THE SWING ERA, 1939-40).

Stan Kenton's *Rockin'* starts out in Ellington style with the vocalist (originally June Christy, re-created here by Eileen Wilson) keeping herself and the band relaxed during the first chorus. Trombones, then saxes give her low-toned backing; a trumpet and a tenor sax wail with her for a while. The band screams its feeling, but the girl returns to quiet things down. Such torchy songs were not Kenton's stock-in-trade. But this version, arranged by Gene Roland, the innovator of the unique saxophone sound heard in Woody Herman's *Four Brothers* on Side 4 of this album, manages to keep the blues feeling while still giving Stan a chance to put his customary weight into the orchestration.

Band 5 ALL OF ME
Billy May version

The old torch song was never treated so wittily as it was by Billy May when he led his big band in the 1950s—an occasion he re-creates here as leader of THE SWING ERA's band. The May trademark is impressed on the piece right off, the saxes "leaning" into the melody with drawn-out notes and expert swipes. The brass makes interjections, the beat takes little skips, the shrill trumpets are countered by smooth trombones. Brass echoes the saxes, which try another phrase that the trombones then take up in a different key. Trombones play warmly beneath the thin trumpets, then a tenor sax plays lightly around the trombone lead. After the brass, the leaning saxes return and the band, stuttering for a moment, winds up.

Gerald Marks, a distinguished veteran of American popular music, wrote *All of Me* (his other unforgettable song was *Is It True What They Say About Dixie?*) in 1931 while playing piano at a summer resort in Harbor Springs, Mich. "Later on," he says, "I was playing in a gambling place in Detroit when Seymour Simons came in. I played it for him, and he wrote a lot of lines for it. We picked the ones we liked best, and I took the song to New York. But nobody wanted it because 'it was dirty.' The words 'Why not take all of me?' was a big departure at the time. One publisher asked: 'Would you sing this to your mother?' and I replied: 'Not if I had your mind,' and I picked up the manuscript and took the train back home. . . . Belle Baker, the famous vaudeville star, was playing at the Fisher Theater, and Seymour and I went over with our song. She said we could play it while she put on her makeup. There was a small café-size piano in her room, so I sat down and played while Simons and I sang. Belle put her head down on the dressing table and proceeded to cry and cry. We stopped, but she lifted her head and said, 'Don't stop.' Mascara was all over her face.

"Well, Belle tried it out at a matinee with me in the pit at the piano and took seven encores. And as she sang it, she cried. When she got back to New York she sang it on a Saturday-night radio interview program, and Monday morning every store in New York had calls for *All of Me*. It was a hit just like that.

"The song raised Belle's salary about a thousand a week. I asked her why she cried so much when she first heard it. She told me: 'That was the first date I played after burying my husband three weeks before,' and I realized that the words 'Can't you see I'm no good without you. Take my lips, I want to lose them' must have been very difficult for her. She sang it for the rest of her life, and at every performance she cried.

"Belle died many years later, and I was a little late getting to her funeral. The only seat left was way down by the organ, which was playing all of Belle's songs. It was just finishing *Say It Isn't So*, and as I started down the aisle it went into *All of Me*. That walk to my seat seemed miles long. The audience saw what was happening, and afterward someone remarked to me, 'Well, what a songwriter will do for a plug!'"

SIDE TWO

Band 1 APRIL IN PARIS
Count Basie version

As Vernon Duke told it in his autobiography, *Passport to Paris*, he was writing the score for a revue called *Walk a Little Faster* back in 1932 and "after auditioning same particularly untalented girls, we all repaired to Tony's; the 'we' consisting of Dorothy Parker, Evelyn Hoey, Robert Benchley, Monty Woolley. . . Evelyn was to be entrusted with the singing chores in the new musical. After several double Scotches, we all got pretty sentimental. I can't think whether it was Benchley or Woolley who cried out: 'Oh to be in Paris now that April's here!' The rest went off in true Class B musical picture fashion. 'April in Paris,' said I melodramatically, 'What a title! My kingdom for a piano!' No sooner were these words uttered than the ever obliging Tony ventured the information that an old wretched upright was at my disposal on the second floor. The piano was wretched indeed, but it made appropriate sounds when persuaded and using the title 'April in Paris' for what they call the 'front phrase' in the trade, I soon completed the reasonably immortal refrain."

Oblivion, not immortality, seemed its likely fate. When the show opened, Broadway critics ignored the song—except for one who said it seemed superfluous. But *April in Paris* was taken up by chanteuses in sophisticated nightclubs, widened its popularity and became as reasonably immortal as any of Duke's songs, such as *I Can't Get Started, Taking a Chance on Love* or *Cabin in the Sky*.

The Basie version, which was arranged by organist Wild Bill Davis, is a little cavalier with the song—more amused by than moved by it. After a respectful first chorus, the fun starts with the trumpet (Thad Jones in the original) trying *Pop Goes the Weasel* in two different keys. The band works the melody over and, with trumpets reaching and drums pounding, goes into a portentous finale. Now comes a stunt that was worked out when Basie and Davis were both playing at Birdland in New York City in the '50s. Davis would play *April* with his trio, then turn to Basie and say: "One more time" and Basie's band would play it. This developed into what is now known as the *One-more-time-April-in-Paris*. After the finale, a voice (Basie's originally, re-created here by the Count's old deputy leader Marshal Royal) calls for more; drums and brass steam into another drawn-out finale; a pause, the voice asks for still more; and another elaborate ending. This is the final finale in Basie's recorded version, but sometimes, in performance, the endings would go on and on. In fact, on a telethon once, the band did it 127 more times.

Band 2 THE CONTINENTAL
Tommy Dorsey version

Guy Holden (Fred Astaire), a dancer, falls for Mimi (Ginger Rogers), a geologist's wife who is trying to divorce her husband. As the movie, *The Gay Divorcee*, unfolds, Fred pursues Ginger, makes off with her, and winds up on a half-acre dance floor with her in his arms, wings on his feet and a Latin ballad in the air: "It has a passion, the Continental, an invitation to moonlight and romance. It's quite the fashion, the Continental, because you tell of your love while you dance." And off they go into one of the unforgettable Astaire-Rogers dance numbers. *The Continental* provided the high point of the movie, and it was the first song to win an Academy Award.

Bill Finegan, the gifted arranger, gave it a sophisticated setting, full of complex countermelodies. A tense opening is followed by a quiet statement of a theme. Trombones in harmony intone the melody, the ensemble shouts it and a dulcet trombone sings it. The band plays a mix of harmonies and rhythms, loud passages alternate with soft, a few simple swinging bars provide a respite, and the strident ensemble end is upstaged by three little piccolo toots.

Oh, yes, Fred convinces Ginger that he is as lovable as he is light-footed, and they dance happily ever after.

Band 3 EARLY AUTUMN
Woody Herman version

In 1946 Ralph Burns, Woody Herman's composer-arranger, wrote a three-part suite called *Summer Sequence*. He later wrote a Part IV but, because the suite was already long, that last part was always played as a separate piece called *Early Autumn*. It is full of musical mists, seasonal wistfulness and beautiful saxophone sounds. In the first chorus, the sax section plays with a warm-toned detachment, and the alto (originally Woody Herman) takes off in the style of Duke Ellington's great Johnny Hodges. The vibraphone provides a clear-toned contrast to the reeds, the saxes respond with ever-deepening tones. Then comes the tenor saxophone solo that made both piece and performer famous: the chorus played originally by Stan Getz, who has become one of the most popular figures of the newer forms of jazz and a leading influence on all of today's saxophonists. His tenor (re-created by Justin Gordon) comes on assertively in *Early Autumn,* turns cool but romantic as it carries the melody with light phrases and lingers briefly on the notes. The brass and other saxes ease in and out, then the tenor is back, darker now in tone, brushing the falling cadences into a hesitant end.

Band 4 THE CHAMP
Ted Heath version

"I think," says Dizzy Gillespie, trying to recall the history of his composition, "that *The Champ* was named for somebody, but I don't know who." Dave Usher, the noted trumpeter's old friend and partner, fills in this lapse of memory. "A week or so before we recorded it," he says, "Dizzy was appearing at the Apollo in Harlem. The disc jockey who was emceeing used to clown around with Dizzy, and as Dizzy was to be introduced the M.C. poked him onstage with a gesture that Dizzy didn't think appropriate. He was vexed, and when he came offstage after the performance, Dizzy took one punch at the M.C. and laid him out flat. I think I said: 'Jeez, man, you're the champ'

and when we recorded the number, we gave it that title. I remember that Ted Heath was one of the first to record it after we did."

The Heath version starts with some feints by the ensemble, a lot of fancy footwork by the drum and piano, and a nice exchange of jabs by a couple of tenor saxes. The trombones do some counterpunching, the brass swings wildly and, after a long windup, the brass lets go with a roundhouse.

The Champ is an impressive exhibition by the best British big band of the time, one whose discipline and spirit reflected the influence of Glenn Miller. Heath started as a trombonist, performing as a child in band concerts in South London. Later, when times were tough, he "busked" in the streets, playing for the pennies that passers-by dropped in his hat.

What happened next could happen only in a sentimental British pantomime. Heath was playing outside Queens Hall Roof Gardens one night when Jack Hylton, the famous impresario and bandleader, came by. Hylton's trombone player had just quit and, hearing Heath, Hylton gave him a trial. Naturally Ted made good and, after a struggle, wound up leading his own band. In the 1950s he drew the kind of crowds at the London Palladium that Benny Goodman and Tommy Dorsey used to draw at the Paramount in New York in the 1930s. He became known, of course, as "Mr. Music" and "The King of Swing." A regular and welcome visitor to the U.S., Heath was the first British leader to give a jazz concert at Carnegie Hall. On his American tours, critics praised his band for its "spotless precision and wild eruptions."

Band 5 SO RARE
Jimmy Dorsey version

After their long and bitter separation, the Dorsey brothers had been reconciled (as told in the 1941-42 album of THE SWING ERA) and were playing together again. In the fall of 1956, Jimmy got together a pickup band, recruited largely from Tommy's band, to make a few sides for a small record company named Fraternity. He included *So Rare,* an old standard.

As Harry Carlson, president of Fraternity, recalls it: "Jimmy played a real honky-tonk sax over a kind of rock rhythm. I said: 'I think that's something younger people will accept.' But after hearing the playback, Jimmy asked me not to release it. 'I play sophisticated sax,' he said. 'No one will recognize me.' And when Tommy heard it, he said: 'I think it's the worst record Jimmy ever made.' But I released it and in the first two weeks got orders for just 25 records. I got all the radio stations in Cincinnati, where we were located, to give it a big play, and I got orders for 30,000 in Cincinnati alone. It went on from there to be Jimmy's biggest hit ever."

Neal Hefti, who was conductor for the session, remembers that "Carlson said everything in the arrangement was too sweet and could I hypo it? I changed it so what had been soft was loud, and Jimmy was to play real rough. Tommy hated it so much. He felt that anyone who bastardized the Dorsey sound should have something done to him physically. I immediately turned all the responsibility over to Carlson, as any red-blooded coward would do."

Rough and honky-tonk it may have sounded to the Dorseys, but *So Rare* is as gutsy a piece as Jimmy's alto sax ever played and, despite the rock, as full of jazz feeling. The alto sax (re-created here by Skeets Herfurt) rolls into the melody, pauses impatiently for the vocalists and comes back strong, embellishing the theme with little lyric licks and finishing with a skillful cadenza.

By the time the record was released, Tommy had died and Jimmy was mortally ill with lung cancer. He did not live to accept the gold record marking the millionth sale of *So Rare.* "But," says Carlson, "I used to see Jimmy in the hospital and *So Rare* was No. 1 on all the programs. Jimmy insisted on having a radio in his room and though he couldn't speak, when he heard it, he would smile."

Band 1 ST. LOUIS BLUES MARCH
Glenn Miller version

The original Glenn Miller recording of this was made in 1943 when Captain Glenn Miller of the U.S. Army Air Corps was leading a band for the aviation cadet parades at Yale. Recorded as a V-disc, made only for the armed forces, St. Louis Blues March was not released as a commercial record until 1955.

The idea of making a march out of St. Louis Blues occurred to Ray McKinley, the noted drummer and bandleader who joined the Air Corps and was assigned to one of Miller's outfits. "We were a drum-and-bugle corps and when we went into retreat, we used to play the usual drum stuff," says Ray. "I got the idea of jazzing it up a bit and, one day, Perry Burgett, my old arranger, and I were lying on the grass and I started to sing a blues march. Perry wrote it down—you know with a good arranger you don't need a piano. It was two bars each of brass and drums. Glenn liked the idea and commissioned Jerry Gray to write an arrangement for his big orchestra. Our stuff was used for parade and was very successful, though a couple of the boys started swinging too much as they marched and got gigged."

It wouldn't be fair to punish anyone for breaking out of strict march time when this St. Louis Blues was played. The drummer throughout keeps an obedient martial beat, breaking into ruffles and rolls without ever bending the 4/4 time. But the rest of the musicians lapse into jazzy fanfares and swing licks, syncopate when they can get away with it, and even drop in a little Blues in the Night.

Such novel marching tunes annoyed Glenn Miller's military superiors. Miller coolly out-brassed the brass and shrugged off the objections. He went on, in fact, to horrify headquarters even further by swinging the sacrosanct marches of John Philip Sousa. "Anybody," he said when complaints came in, "anybody can improve on Sousa."

Band 2 THE PEANUT VENDOR
Stan Kenton version .

This is the song that brought the rumba and Cuban rhythm to popularity in the U.S., an unassuming melody over a hitching beat with words that were as far from the June-moon tradition of American pop music as it's possible to get—"Peanuts! If you haven't got bananas don't be blue, Peanuts in a little bag are calling you." It was written in 1929 by Moises Simons, a Havana bandleader who was a ranking Cuban composer, along with Ernesto Lecuona (The Breeze and I and Siboney) and Eliseo Grenet (Mama Inez). Herbert Marks, the American music publisher, heard Peanut Vendor in Havana—it was called El Manisero—and imported it in 1930. But U.S. orchestra leaders were very slow to pick it up. Little Latin music had been heard in the U.S. since the tango fad, and Marks had to import claves and maracas to supply the appropriate sound for jazz bands.

Peanut Vendor was originally what the Cubans call a son, a slow and dignified dance tune. That word son on the sheet music confused Americans, who thought it was a typographical error, so the publishers decided to call it a rumba—not because Peanut Vendor was a rumba (which was a very athletic dance), but because rumba was a name Americans had heard before. The success of Peanut Vendor brought a flood of Cuban music to the U.S. and gratification to Señor Simons, who also wrote Marta ("rambling rose of the wildwood") and became a Cuban cultural hero. When he died in 1948, all Havana went into mourning.

The Kenton Peanut Vendor is a tour de force. "Stan dictated notes for it about an hour before we went up on the bandstand for a job," says Bart Varsalona, who played the bass trombone for Kenton. Shelly Manne, the drummer, adds that "every night different musicians would add their little bits until it grew into what it was." And Eddie Safranski, the bass player, remembers that "it became quite involved and everybody joining the band had to learn it by instinct."

The start is straight enough, with the rhythm section augmented by bongo and conga drums and maracas. A wonderful trombone (originally Milt Bernhart, re-created here by Dick Nash) starts its solo, loose at first then strident. Then things begin to build, sound on sound, motion against countermotion, theme over theme, discordance outdoing itself as the brass drowns the reeds, the percussion gets busier and busier, the trumpets pitch themselves higher and higher until the peanut vendor, who ordinarily leaves with a plaintive "Peanuts, I go . . .", stalks off with a shrill protest.

Band 3 LI'L DARLIN'
Count Basie version

By the time he made Li'l Darlin', hard times were ending for Count Basie. When the big band business fell apart in the late 1940s, he organized small groups, simply because he couldn't afford to keep a big band together. "Things were kind of tough for a big band," Basie explained. "People were trying to make up their minds whether they were going to like bop. Nobody was thinking of dancing. But I wasn't too comfortable with a small band. People look for you to be really there, and my piano is on the blues side, not the way they play piano these days. Disc jockeys began to play big band music so I decided to try again. It made me feel better to have a big band."

His new big band finally clicked, musically and financially, by 1954. Of his incomparable old group, only one veteran was back—Freddie Green, the guitarist. His sidemen of the '30s and '40s had been accustomed to improvisation and his repertory had been, says Basie, "a whole book full of heads." His sidemen of the '50s played basically from arrangements, taking liberties but not going completely off the reservation. Old Basie admirers grumbled that sure they were great but so was a well-oiled machine. They were at home in the new harmonies of jazz, accommodating the taste for bop, says Basie, "by putting the mink coat on the chords."

Li'l Darlin', Neal Hefti's composition, is touched by the new sounds. It starts with a few simple chords, like bells tolling, and the piano all but swoons into the melody. The mood persists, laced with languishing and lovely sounds—the piano and guitar fill-ins, the up-and-over effects by the horns, the tender muted trumpet and the sighing phrases before the final chords.

Band 4 TANGO BLUES
Harry James version

The ending of the Swing Era did not keep Harry James quiet for long. Only a few months after giving up his band at the end of 1946, he was back with another one. "I've settled a few problems," he said, "and I've got me a bunch of kids and their spirit kills me. How can I possibly feel like not blowing!"

He hasn't ever lost that feeling, and when he recorded Tango Blues he broke out in as spectacular a solo as he had ever blown. The idea of doing a blues in tango time was Harry's though it was not original with him. Other blues, notably St. Louis Blues, have a tango treatment. Harry's is dark in texture, as much Latin as jazz. The ensemble sets the mood, the beat changes to a stop-time tango, and the trumpet comes leaping in with a bullring sound, as if calling the crowds to a corrida. The band keeps up the excitement, and the tenor sax plays a beautiful chorus. But the piece belongs to Harry's trumpet (here re-created by Joe Graves). The rhythmic adventurousness is a contrast to the straight-ahead 4/4 of Harry's earlier swing days—willingness to change and grow has made James so irrepressible an artist.

Band 5 CARAVAN
Ralph Marterie version

By a curious coincidence, there are three numbers on this side of the album that take hallowed old standards and give them unexpected, irreverent readings: the melancholy *St. Louis Blues* is done as a brisk march; the wistful *Peanut Vendor* comes out as a dissonant harangue; and here the exotic, languorous *Caravan* is bounced by a loud electric guitar. The original *Caravan* was an Ellington classic (THE SWING ERA, 1936-37) written by Ellington and Juan Tizol, who also played an unforgettable chorus on his soulful valve trombone.

Ralph Marterie's version is a different kettle of camels. The drums set up a chunkety-chunk rhythm and the guitar jumps on the melody. It squeezes in some Bedouin trills, drops out, then resumes its heavy twanging. Sometimes West is East, sometimes it's the other way. In their *Caravan*, Ellington and Tizol tempted you to linger, with hints of veiled beauties and Oriental delights. Marterie never lets his *Caravan*

stray from the no-nonsense business of keeping the camels moving.

A trumpeter who formed his first band when he was in the Navy during World War II, Marterie became for a while as successful as any leader in the business, playing in a style more pop than jazz. His *Caravan*, he thinks, was first played by a combo in Philadelphia—he simply picked it up for a bigger ensemble. A tough boss, Marterie ran his band, as he put it, "like the SAC Air Force runs its organization. I don't care what my musicians say about me. I fire them unless they're on the ball. I hate bad musicians." Though unpopular with his sidemen ("I wouldn't care to comment on him as a person," one said tactfully), he was so big with the public that in 1957 the National Ballroom Operators voted his 17-man band America's No. 1 sweet swing band.

SIDE FOUR

Band 1 FOUR BROTHERS
Woody Herman version

Few bandleaders have changed so radically and lasted so long as Woody Herman. His first group was the easygoing Band That Plays the Blues, which played from 1936 to 1941 and is represented in THE SWING ERA re-creations by such numbers as *Blue Flame* (1941-42 album) and *Blues on Parade* (1940-41 album). In 1944 Herman formed his hard-driving First Herd, whose work is re-created in THE SWING ERA's 1944-45 and *Postwar Years* albums. His Second Herd, which is re-created in this album, played with a nonchalant sophistication. Later there was a Third Herd and after that so many others that Woody once exclaimed: "I feel as if there had been 80!"

Four Brothers was the Second Herd's most famous number, establishing a new use of saxophones in swing. The brothers were the featured members of the saxophone section, three tenors and a baritone. The idea of emphasizing this combination originated with arranger Gene Roland, whose idea was brought to Herman by Jimmy Guiffre, himself a noted reed man, composer and teacher. As Guiffre tells it: "Gene was in New York in the late '40s and would hang out at a place called Nola Studios where all the bands rehearsed and musicians met. For some reason, there were a lot of good tenor players around, there must have been a hundred of them. The usual sax section at the time was two altos, two tenors, one bari. Gene decided to write a four-tenor sax piece. He liked the sound very much and everybody did. When he came out to Los Angeles, we got together a band with four tenors. When Woody was forming his Second Herd he hired three tenors from the group: Stan Getz, Zoot Sims and Herbie Steward, and got Serge Chaloff from another group. Woody said to me: 'Why don't you write a piece featuring the four-sax sound?' I did and called it 'Four Mothers.' Woody changed it to *Four Brothers*. It took months before the band could play it right. Though it's a four-tenor sound, Herman didn't use four tenors, so it was played by his three tenors and a baritone. He later used the four brothers sound all through his Third Herd repertory."

In *Four Brothers*, the saxes come in together on the fetching melody with a hard-reed sound that manages to sound both cool and warm at the same time. Trumpets and drums hit the accents. Then come the brothers, one by one. First, in the original, was Zoot Sims (Justin Gordon in this re-creation), booting the theme. Next was Serge Chaloff (re-created by Bill Perkins), reaching with his supple baritone into the lower registers. Herbie Steward, the light-fingered brother (re-created by Don Lodice), is next, and then Stan Getz (re-created by Don Raffell) with his airy romantic touches. For a while, the saxophones keep more to the background, changing in texture from thick to open. And at the end, each of the brothers comes in for a two-bar break.

Band 2 V.I.P.'S BOOGIE
Duke Ellington version

The Duke has written hundreds of tunes, and when he was asked recently about *V.I.P.'s Boogie* he couldn't at the moment recall

it. He asked some of his sidemen about it, and Harry Carney, his baritone sax, reminded him: "It's the one we always played with *Jam with Sam*. It starts out with my solo—the first part is sort of like a cadenza."

Carney's cadenza comes in with a thick blues texture that he carries on into a solo as the beat goes into a boogie. After the saxes and brass, the clarinet (Jimmy Hamilton originally, re-created by Gus Bivona), which has been wandering around over the trumpets, comes in to whirl and twist up into a series of licks that usher in the final chord. Boogie was never an Ellington specialty, and the piano gets in very few boogie licks. In fact, as the piece goes on it becomes more Ellington than boogie, especially in its harmonies. "That Ellington," says Louis Bellson, the drummer whose rhythms drove the piece along, "he voices those saxophones so great that five of them sound as if there were nine."

Band 3 ACROSS THE ALLEY FROM THE ALAMO
Stan Kenton version

This marriage of happy-go-lucky tune and morbid lyric calls for an explanation—and Joe Greene, its author, provides one that makes everything clear. "I'd just been in an auto wreck," he begins, "and my arm was in a sling. One night I had a weird dream where I saw the whole thing like in a film—the Alamo, the tepee, the Indian. I couldn't write so I woke my wife and went to the piano. I sketched out the tune with one hand while she wrote it down.

"Next morning I had an appointment with a talent agent. I sang him a couple of tunes I had and he didn't like them, so I told him I had written a kind of hillbilly song, a tongue-in-cheek sort of thing. He liked it, and we made a demo and sent it to Tommy Rockwell, the big agent. On Wednesday, Woody Herman walked into Rockwell's office and listened to it. He got hold of an arranger and recorded it that night. Thursday morning the Mills Brothers were in a recording session and Rockwell phoned me for another chorus. I dashed it off and sang it to him over the phone. Friday night Herman's record was on the air and about a week after I wrote it, it was a smash hit."

At that time, Stan Kenton was on a serious jazz kick, and *Across the Alley from the Alamo* was not the kind of music he was really interested in. But another lugubrious song also written by Joe Greene, *And Her Tears Flowed Like Wine*, had been a whopping moneymaker for him and he was talked into doing *Alamo*. Arranger Pete Rugolo gave it a very straightforward treatment—"We didn't try to scare anybody with it," he explains. After a tom-tom opening and some raspy trombones, the vocalist (June Christy's part is here sung by Eileen Wilson) cheerfully recounts the doleful story of the inattentive Indian and his hapless horse.

Band 4 BINGO, BANGO, BOFFO
Tommy Dorsey version

The riff on which *Bingo, Bango, Boffo* is based is simple, but a lot of things happen around it. Sticks on the high-hat cymbal lead into muted trumpets, which play the tight little theme over some hand-clapping. Saxes move in, followed by trumpets, trombones and an emphatic solo trumpet (originally Charlie Shavers, re-created here by Pete Candoli). With an old swing beat and some interesting key changes, *Bingo* moves from tenor sax to piano fill-ins to light trombones and saxes. The muted trumpets come back, the trombones do pull-ups beneath the saxes, and the windup is capped by a flurry of drums.

"I brought this in to Tommy without a title," says composer-arranger Bill Finegan, "and he came up with *Bingo, Bango, Boffo*. Tommy liked things on the high-pressure side, and this is a noisy piece with plenty going on. So the title seemed appropriate."

Band 5 LEAN BABY
Billy May version
Through the 1930s and '40s trumpeter Billy May earned a reputation as one of the best arrangers in swing—he did *Cherokee* and *Pompton Turnpike* for Charlie Barnet, *Ida* for Glenn Miller, dozens of numbers for Bing Crosby and Frank Sinatra and others. Some thought that if Billy would pay less attention to arranging and a little more to

his trumpet playing, he would have few rivals on the horn. Then in 1951 Billy took on another career. Capitol Records got him to lead a band in some sides that mixed the contemporary dance style with the old hard-driving Jimmie Lunceford beat.

The two May numbers in this album came out of this session —*All of Me* (played on Side 1) and May's biggest song hit, *Lean Baby*. This latter number starts out with his "leaning saxes" complaining against a gutty Lunceford rhythm. The melody moves from section to section. The tenor sax does a graceful turn, the piano has some locked-hand passages (both hands playing the same chords in unison), the trombones play together. A drum break starts up all the brass as the cymbals accent the second and fourth beats. Then saxes come on as if they were starting all over, but suddenly they—and everything else —stop.

Lean Baby was both composed and arranged by May, and the idea in the title was "Baby, lean on me." Roy Alfred wrote some lyrics about, in May's words, "a skinny broad." This displeased May, but when Frank Sinatra sang them, says May, "he sold so many records I had to like it." But, he adds, "I'm still sore about the lyric."

SIDE FIVE

Band 1 HOT TODDY
Ralph Flanagan version
Both Ralph Flanagan as a bandleader and *Hot Toddy*, his theme song, were accidents. Flanagan was enjoying his career as a top-notch arranger in the late 1940s when Victor started looking around for somebody to emulate the Glenn Miller sound for their records. When Flanagan's name was proposed, the story goes, a Victor executive thought it was Finegan—Bill Finegan, whose work is heard in this SWING ERA album in the Tommy Dorsey and Sauter-Finegan numbers. Before the misconception could be cleared up, Flanagan was hired—and afterward nobody cared. The big, disciplined sound Flanagan got from his band was such a success that dealers could not keep his records in stock.

Hot Toddy, Flanagan recalls, "was recorded by chance only because we had a few minutes left over on a recording date. Like all arrangers, I had a few things lying around in a briefcase, and this was one of them. Didn't even have a name for it, but somebody thought up *Hot Toddy*. Its success was a surprise to everybody."

It is probably the hypnotic simplicity, the cheerful galumphing of the beat that makes *Hot Toddy* so attractive. The three-note melody, played over a stubborn rhythm, comes out first on the piano and hardly ever goes away. Shrilling trumpets try to break things up but give in quietly to the theme and to the beat.

Flanagan was a bandleader for only a few years. "I hated fronting the band," he admits today. "Hated the travel and the one-night stands and the hotel living." Retired and happy to be out of it, he devotes himself now to studying classical piano.

Band 2 THE DOODLETOWN FIFERS
Sauter-Finegan version
"There has never been so much equipment for a SWING ERA session," wrote correspondent Barbara Wilkins in her report to TIME-LIFE RECORDS, "as was hauled out to re-create Sauter-Finegan's *Doodle-town Fifers*. There was a harp, a tuba, drums in all sizes from snare to parade, an acoustic guitar, an electric guitar. Two saxophonists played piccolos. One sideman played the triangle. Six of them doubled on finger cymbals, and the whole band whistled."

Such instrumentation was typical of the Sauter-Finegan band. Eddie Sauter and Bill Finegan had been two of the finest arrangers and composers in swing before they formed their band in 1952 and set new standards in boldness, inventiveness—and humor. Certainly there has been no more elaborate or successful piece of swing whimsy than

The Doodletown Fifers, which transmutes the famous old *The Year of Jubilo* into something halfway between a fife-and-drum corps and an out-of-its-mind symphony orchestra. The introduction might be described as a fanfare—trumpets, trombones, a silvery triangle, running saxes and parade-style drums. Over the drums comes the fife with the familiar theme. Saxes take the melody over a crowd of percussion instruments and, as the thin sound of distant trumpets is heard, trombones march in. From here on it's hard to sift the sounds—trombones barking, trumpets calling, saxes falling, drums rolling, tuba puffing, fife fifing . . .

The composers took the name from a village outside New York City not far from where Sauter lived. They took their tune from a famous Civil War song, *Kingdom Coming*, also known as *The Year of Jubilo*, which was written by Henry Clay Work, a printer who learned to write songs by playing on a melodeon he found in a Hartford, Conn., printshop. Work had strong feelings about two things: slavery and drinking. In 1862 he wrote the first of several popular abolitionist songs, *Kingdom Coming*, a slave's vision of what freedom would bring: "Say, darkies, hab you seen de massa Wid de muffstas on his face, Go 'long de road sometime dis mornin' Like he gwine to leab de place? He seen a smoke way up de ribber, Whar the Linkum gumboats lay; He took his hat an lef' berry sudden, An I spec he's run away! De massa run, ha! ha! De darkies stay, ho! ho! It mus' be now de kingdom comin' An' de year ob Jubilo!"

Later Work wrote another tune that became even more famous, *Marching Through Georgia*. The Union soldiers loved it, but General William Tecumseh Sherman, whose feat it celebrates, always felt that the song took attention away from his other military achievements and once declared that "if I had thought when I made that march that it would have inspired anyone to compose a piece, I would have marched *around* the state."

To express his feeling on the evils of drinking, Work composed a song that was sung in the celebrated play, *Ten Nights in a Bar-room*—for a scene in which the daughter pushes aside the swinging doors of the saloon and in a quavering voice breaks into what has become the most widely known and widely parodied of all temperance songs: "Father, dear father, come home with me now."

Band 3 INTERLUDE
Stan Kenton version
"When the Kenton band would play hotels," reports Pete Rugolo, who was not only Kenton's arranger but his alter ego, "people were always screaming that the band was too loud. I wrote this little

piece for Stan to play to still the screams. It was only five trombones, bass, guitar, piano and drums—no trumpets, no saxes. Stan's still playing it with his present orchestra—it's been a nice thing for him."

The piano opens with arpeggios and then, in the soft swish of brushes on snare, the distinctive rhythm of *Interlude*—with its soft little halt—leads into the sad-sweet melody. The trombones come in as background, then offer a countermelody. In a little transition, the beat changes. When piano and trombones engage in dialogue, it turns almost unnoticed back to the original tempo.

Kenton, who is liked and admired by almost everybody who ever worked for him, has no greater admirer than Rugolo, who was with him for years before leaving to go on his own. "I guess," Rugolo once said, "that an arranger's idea of paradise is some place where he can write anything he wants to and still manage to make a living. That's why I felt like I was walking through the pearly gates when I went to work with Stan Kenton. Not only could I arrange the way I wanted to, but I could even compose originals and know they'd be heard. To make the situation more unbelievable, Stan never said, 'Don't do it this way' or 'Don't do it that way.' He was willing to try anything so long as he felt the writer really meant what he was saying."

Band 4 CUTE
Count Basie version

The flute, now a familiar instrument in contemporary jazz, took a long time to break into swing. Benny Carter and Chick Webb had used it in their 1930s bands, and Jimmie Lunceford tried it. But not until the early '50s did it really gain acceptance. Even then, most of its players did not think it fitted into big band swing. One who did was Frank Wess, Basie's tenor sax player, who doubled on flute and showed off its lovely tones in the second chorus of *Cute*.

Wess never pampered the flute, which has a reputation for being delicate. In *Cute* it cuts the notes sharply, swinging as easily as if it were a clarinet and stealing the show for a while from the drums. The drums (originally Sonny Payne, re-created here by Nick Fatool), which have had everything their way in the first chorus, come back for a showy solo, let the saxes buzz off into some riffs, then erupt through the rest of the piece—although the flute gets in the last toot.

Neal Hefti, who composed *Cute*, was·a main reason for the success of Basie's new big band. (He also wrote two other Basie numbers played in this album: *The Kid from Red Bank* and *Li'l Darlin'*.)

Famous for his work with Woody Herman's First Herd (his *Good Earth* is re-created in THE SWING ERA, *The Postwar Years*, and *Wildroot* in the 1944-45 album), he was working on his own when Basie asked him to do some arrangements in 1950. Hefti did, and wound up becoming Basie's chief arranger. "Basie never bruised my music," he says. "His men would add things of their own, but they respected the fact that I had written it and had a certain thing in mind."

Neal Hefti's direct musical style matched up well with Basie's own straightforward musical instincts. Hefti has always chosen simple but never obvious ways of solving problems, stayed fresh in his approach without being far out. Most of all for a leader like Basie, whose rhythm section was his special pride, he had a way with 4/4 time that as critic Whitney Balliett put it, "put wheels on all four beats."

Band 5 PUSSY WILLOW
Tommy Dorsey version

The whole band purrs through *Pussy Willow*. The saxophones flow into the first chorus with the trombones speaking in legato whispers. When the trumpets run down a whole-tone scale, the trombones carry the scale along. The murmuring saxes come back, the trombones play a lovely high-register come-on for the tenor sax, and muted trumpets end the last chorus with a hanging thread of spun-glass sound. "I named this one myself," says composer Bill Finegan. "It was spring, and there's a theme in the introduction that says 'pussy willow.'"

Tommy Dorsey never got better ensemble work from any of his bands than he did from this one, the last of his great groups. It was kept together not just by affection for Tommy but by respect for him, a respect tinged with fear. "I used to call him the wonderful tyrant—you had to respect him whether you liked him or not," says Charlie Shavers, trumpeter in this band. "He couldn't stand incompetents. He was sadistic with them. He had a kid couldn't play much piano, but he wouldn't fire him, just made his life miserable. Maybe that was his way of getting him to be a plumber. He fired me once in Lake Tahoe and wouldn't give me carfare home. In 1947 I was playing in Milwaukee, and he came through and came over to hear me, and he said: 'When ya comin' home, ya big jerk?' So I came back. Once we really came up to a fight. I said: 'Let's go out in the alley,' and we went out and took our jackets off and squared off, and then we looked at each other and both of us broke out laughing."

Band 1 ARTISTRY JUMPS
Stan Kenton version

Through his years as a bandleader, Stan Kenton has remained very attached to his first theme song, *Artistry in Rhythm* (THE SWING ERA, *The Postwar Years*), not just out of sentiment but because it was so inextricably identified with him. He used the name and sometimes the theme, which is reminiscent of Romberg's *Softly as in a Morning Sunrise*, in seven other pieces—*Artistry in Bass*, *Artistry in Bolero*, *Artistry in Percussion*, *Artistry in Boogie*, *Artistry in Harlem Swing*, *Artistry in Tango* and in *Artistry Jumps*, the first of the series of *Artistry* sequels. *Artistry in Rhythm* played the theme broadly, for the most part, over a stately rhythm. *Artistry Jumps* pushes it along as a presto.

The bass speeds off on a fast syncopated rhythm and never slows down—or lets anyone else in the band do so .The piano plays the *Artistry* theme first; then the unison saxes sneak up on it and the brass whangs in. The ensemble mélange that follows ends in whimpering trumpets. A ripe tenor (originally Vido Musso, re-created by Justin Gordon) rides over the rhythm section, which carries *Artistry* to the bursting end.

Band 2 NIGHT TRAIN
Buddy Morrow version

Moe Zudekoff was one of the most respected trombonists of the Swing Era. After attending the Juilliard School of Music in the 1930s, he played for Artie Shaw, Bunny Berigan, Paul Whiteman, both Dorseys and Bob Crosby. Along the way he changed his name to Muni Morrow and finally to Buddy Morrow.

In the early '50s, the Victor recording company, which had launched Ralph Flanagan (whose *Hot Toddy* is re-created on Side 5 of this album) as a successor to Glenn Miller, proposed that Buddy Morrow form a band to reproduce the Tommy Dorsey sound. But whereas Glenn Miller was gone from the scene, Tommy Dorsey was very much around and playing very well. "There wasn't the same nostalgia," explains Morrow.

His band was first-rate, but his tour ended with Morrow $125,000 in the red and ready to break up his band. As a last gesture, he recorded *Night Train*. "I asked a friend, 'How should we play this kind of blues?'" says Morrow, "and he said, 'Play it ignorant,' meaning forget all about my Juilliard training. From then on, it's really a Horatio

Alger story. We made it in one take and it was No. 1 on Victor's list for almost a year, and between the record and the one-nighters it brought us, I paid off the debt."

In the Morrow *Night Train*, the Swing Era met the rock era and the result was a standoff. A compelling triplet rhythm lumbers through the whole number. The trombone wails the melody, followed by heavy saxes and shrill trumpets and, unexpectedly, by a round-toned trombone feelingly played in the original by Morrow. The heavy beat comes back again as *Night Train* pounds to the end.

When Morrow recorded the theme, he did not realize that it had been taken virtually intact from Duke Ellington's *Happy-Go-Lucky Local* (THE SWING ERA, *The Postwar Years*). "It was just another blues to me," says Morrow. "Years later, we played it at the University of Michigan opposite Duke. Before we played *Night Train*, I told the audience that when I first recorded it I didn't know it was part of Duke's sequence, but I was proud to be connected in any way with anything of Ellington's. The Duke told me later that it was almost the first time he was ever close to tears."

Band 3 KEEN AND PEACHY
Woody Herman version
"Sure, *Keen and Peachy* does sound like *Fine and Dandy*," admits Woody Herman. "It's based on the same chords." Ralph Burns, who wrote the piece, amplifies: "Woody told me, couldn't we think about something that is in the same mood as the Kay Swift tune. We didn't want to steal but get the same bounce, the same rhythm and still belong to our time. So I wrote it, and we played around with it. Soon people clamored for it on the dance floor, mainly because of Stan Getz being so great."

Keen and Peachy is definitely of its time, showing brilliantly how swing could absorb the feeling of the new jazz while still remaining swing. After the cool riff on which the number is based is taken alternately by saxes and brass, the first tenor sax solo (Getz originally) comes on. Hard, almost impersonal, but pretty, it carries along over brass exhortations and drum shots. The second, shorter tenor sax solo (Zoot Sims originally) is lighter and warmer. After the trombone's fleet passage, another of the famous four brother saxes comes in, this time the lush baritone (Serge Chaloff originally). Then comes a brilliant passage with trumpets and trombones competing in a complex piece of counterpoint. The trumpet finally breaks into the open for a solo that moves high up into the finale. All through *Keen and Peachy* can be heard a new style of drumming (Don Lamond in the original) that, without making the drum a solo instrument, emphasizes its role as beat-keeper with an exhilarating run of accents, shots and outbursts.

Band 4 STAR BURST
Gene Krupa version
"My original theme song," explains Gene Krupa, "was *Apurksody*. Then we switched to *Drummin' Man*. In 1947, when we were going to open at the old Capitol Theater in New York, I asked

Eddie Finckel, our arranger, to make up just enough music to give us time to get all the way up as the movie-theater pit rose. He came in with the melody of *Star Burst*, and we used it for a while as our introductory theme. The head of Columbia Records liked the theme and said, 'Record it.' So later Dick Taylor embellished it some more and this is how it came out. Then, just for a gag, we added that little sign-off, the thing we always played to tell the dancers the set was over."

Star Burst is a suave piece with interesting changes of keys and tempo. It starts off fast and big—drums and trumpet chords—but suddenly slows, sweeping into the melody. Back it goes into double time, the wiry trumpet and the drums making their points skillfully and briefly. Back again to the slow time, the trumpet leading the ensemble and the trombones going it alone. And then the it's-all-over bit.

Eddie Finckel explains the title. "I'm an astronomy fan, and at my place in the country I'd been keeping track of meteor showers for years. One night I went out and saw a spectacular shower, and the sight of this glorious heavenly display suggested *Star Burst*. I really think the opening phrases do suggest a fire show."

Band 5 BENJIE'S BUBBLE
Benny Goodman version
When he first played this number, Goodman gave it its rightful name, *Under the Double Eagle*. But he changed it to honor his younger daughter Benjie. Only the year before he had named a piece after her sister—*Rachel's Dream* (THE SWING ERA, *The Postwar Years*). The familiar *Under the Double Eagle* march is remembered by most people as having been written by John Philip Sousa, who gave it such rousing performances. But he didn't write it. An Austrian bandmaster named Josef Franz Wagner did, patriotically naming it after the two-headed emblem of Austria.

Benjie's Bubble was arranged for Goodman by Joe Bushkin, one of swing's most skillful and scholarly pianists, and in it Benny himself did some beautiful bubbling. After saxes and trumpets have marched in, the clarinet (re-created here by Abe Most) dances over the parade, marking time on one lick and sounding as if it were about to cut into the old New Orleans classic, *High Society*. The piano (Joe Bushkin in the original) hardly touches ground as it goes, but the drums bring everybody back to the business of marching. With brass busy and drums rolling, *Benjie's Bubble* floats off with a flourish.

The drummer who kept taking charge was Louis Bellson, just about the busiest percussion man of his time. A spectacular technician, Bellson introduced the idea of using two bass drums instead of one in jazz bands and devised the mechanism that enabled one drummer to handle both. He was sought after by virtually every bandleader, and in this album alone he is represented in pieces by Tommy Dorsey and Duke Ellington, as well as Goodman. Married today to Pearl Bailey and heading his own band, Bellson lovingly recalls the swing days: "Every one of those bands was so marvelous. Every one was a joy. There's no way to express in words what I felt about those days. If my end had come the next minute, I would have lived such a beautiful life."

—JOSEPH KASTNER

The Musicians Who Made the Recordings in This Volume

THE KID FROM RED BANK
LEADER: Billy May TRUMPETS: Ray Triscari, Shorty Sherock, John Best, Uan Rasey TROMBONES: Joe Howard, Dick Nash, Dick Noel SAXOPHONES: Marshal Royal, Abe Most, Justin Gordon, Don Raffell, Bill Perkins PIANO: Ray Sherman GUITAR: Jack Marshall BASS: Rolly Bundock DRUMS: Nick Fatool SOLO: Ray Sherman (piano)

SATIN DOLL
LEADER: Billy May TRUMPETS: Pete Candoli, John Audino, John Best, Uan Rasey TROMBONES: Dick Nash, Joe Howard, Lew McCreary SAXOPHONES: Les Robinson, Willie Schwartz, Abe Most, Justin Gordon, Bill Perkins PIANO: Ray Sherman GUITAR: Jack Marshall BASS: Rolly Bundock DRUMS: Nick Fatool SOLOS: Shorty Sherock (trumpet), Ray Sherman (piano)

SWANEE RIVER BOOGIE
LEADER: Glen Gray TRUMPETS: Pete Candoli, Conrad Gozzo, Joe Graves, Manny Klein, Shorty Sherock TROMBONES: Milt Bernhart, Joe How-

ard, Ed Kusby, Dick Noel SAXOPHONES: Gus Bivona, Chuck Gentry, Skeets Herfurt, Julie Jacob, Babe Russin PIANO: Ray Sherman GUITAR: Jack Marshall BASS: Mike Rubin DRUMS: Nick Fatool SOLOS: Pete Candoli (trumpet), Ray Sherman (piano)

JUST A-SITTIN' AND A-ROCKIN'
LEADER: Billy May TRUMPETS: Bud Brisbois, Pete Candoli, John Audino, Ray Triscari, Chuck Findley TROMBONES: Joe Howard, Dick Nash, Lew McCreary, Lloyd Ulyate, Phil Teele

SAXOPHONES: Les Robinson, Abe Most, Justin Gordon, Don Lodice, Bill Perkins PIANO: Ray Sherman GUITAR: Jack Marshall BASS: Rolly Bundock DRUMS: Nick Fatool SOLOS: Chuck Findley (muted trumpet), Bud Brisbois (high trumpet), Justin Gordon (tenor saxophone background to vocal) VOCAL: Eileen Wilson

ALL OF ME
LEADER: Billy May TRUMPETS: John Audino, John Best, Shorty Sherock, Uan Rasey TROMBONES: Joe Howard, Dick Nash, Lew McCreary, Dick Noel SAXOPHONES: Skeets Herfurt, Abe Most, Justin Gordon, Don Raffell, Chuck Gentry PIANO: Ray Sherman GUITAR: Al Hendrickson BASS: Rolly Bundock DRUMS: Nick Fatool SOLO: Don Raffell (tenor saxophone)

APRIL IN PARIS
Same as THE KID FROM RED BANK. SOLOS: Dick Nash (trombone), Pete Candoli (trumpet) VOICE: Marshal Royal

THE CONTINENTAL
LEADER: Billy May TRUMPETS: John Audino, Pete Candoli, Ray Triscari, Uan Rasey, John Best TROMBONES: Joe Howard, Dick Nash, Lew McCreary, Lloyd Ulyate SAXOPHONES: Les Robinson, Willie Schwartz, Don Lodice, Justin Gordon, Chuck Gentry PIANO: Ray Sherman GUITAR: Jack Marshall BASS: Rolly Bundock DRUMS: Nick Fatool SOLOS: Dick Nash (trombone), Pete Candoli (trumpet)

EARLY AUTUMN
LEADER: Billy May TRUMPETS: John Audino, John Best, Shorty Sherock, Uan Rasey, Bud Brisbois TROMBONES: Dick Nash, Joe Howard, Lloyd Ulyate SAXOPHONES: Justin Gordon, Don Lodice, Don Raffell, Bill Perkins PIANO: Ray Sherman GUITAR: Jack Marshall BASS: Rolly Bundock DRUMS: Nick Fatool SOLOS: Les Robinson (alto saxophone), Larry Bunker (vibraphone), Justin Gordon (tenor saxophone)

THE CHAMP
LEADER: Glen Gray TRUMPETS: Pete Candoli, Conrad Gozzo, Manny Klein, Uan Rasey, Shorty Sherock TROMBONES: Milt Bernhart, Joe Howard, Tommy Pederson, George Roberts, Si Zentner SAXOPHONES: Chuck Gentry, Skeets Herfurt, Plas Johnson, Babe Russin, Willie Schwartz PIANO: Ray Sherman GUITAR: George Van Eps BASS: Mike Rubin DRUMS: Nick Fatool SOLOS: Plas Johnson (tenor saxophone), Babe Russin (tenor saxophone), Milt Bernhart (trombone), Joe Howard (trombone), Nick Fatool (drums)

SO RARE
LEADER: Billy May TROMBONES: Dick Nash, Joe Howard, Lloyd Ulyate, Lew McCreary PIANO: Ray Sherman GUITAR: Jack Marshall BASS: Rolly Bundock DRUMS: Nick Fatool SOLO: Skeets Herfurt (alto saxophone) VOCAL GROUP: Sue Allen, Peggy Clark, Ann Clark Terry, Betty Jane Baker, Loulie Jean Norman, William Brown, William Cole, James Wheeler, Jerry Whitman

ST. LOUIS BLUES MARCH
LEADER: Billy May TRUMPETS: John Audino, John Best, Uan Rasey, Shorty Sherock TROMBONES: Joe Howard, Dick Nash, Lew McCreary, Dick Noel SAXOPHONES: Skeets Herfurt, Abe Most, Justin Gordon, Don Raffell, Chuck Gentry PIANO: Ray Sherman GUITAR: Al Hendrickson BASS: Rolly Bundock DRUMS: Nick Fatool SOLOS: Nick Fatool (drums), Skeets Herfurt (alto saxophone)

THE PEANUT VENDOR
LEADER: Billy May TRUMPETS: John Audino, John Best, Shorty Sherock, Uan Rasey, Bud Brisbois TROMBONES: Dick Nash, Joe Howard, Lew McCreary, Lloyd Ulyate, Phil Teele SAXOPHONES: Les Robinson, Abe Most, Don Lodice, Don Raffell, Bill Perkins GUITAR: Jack Marshall

BASS: Rolly Bundock DRUMS: Nick Fatool PERCUSSION: Larry Bunker, Gene Estes, Stan Levey SOLO: Dick Nash (trombone)

LI'L DARLIN'
Same as THE KID FROM RED BANK. SOLO: Pete Candoli (trumpet)

TANGO BLUES
LEADER: Glen Gray TRUMPETS: Conrad Gozzo, Manny Klein, Joe Graves, Shorty Sherock, Uan Rasey TROMBONES: Joe Howard, Lew McCreary, Si Zentner, Milt Bernhart SAXOPHONES: Abe Most, Skeets Herfurt, Plas Johnson, Chuck Gentry, Babe Russin PIANO: Ray Sherman GUITAR: Jack Marshall BASS: Mike Rubin DRUMS: Irv Cottler SOLO: Joe Graves (trumpet)

CARAVAN
LEADER: Billy May TRUMPETS: John Best, Shorty Sherock, John Audino, Uan Rasey TROMBONES: Joe Howard, Dick Nash, Lew McCreary SAXOPHONES: Les Robinson, Willie Schwartz, Justin Gordon, Abe Most, Julie Jacob, Bill Perkins PIANO: Ray Sherman GUITAR: Jack Marshall BASS: Rolly Bundock DRUMS: Nick Fatool SOLO: Bob Bain (guitar)

FOUR BROTHERS
LEADER: Billy May TRUMPETS: John Best, Uan Rasey, Shorty Sherock, John Audino, Bud Brisbois TROMBONES: Dick Nash, Joe Howard, Lloyd Ulyate, Lew McCreary SAXOPHONES: Justin Gordon, Don Raffell, Don Lodice, Bill Perkins PIANO: Ray Sherman GUITAR: Jack Marshall BASS: Rolly Bundock DRUMS: Nick Fatool SOLOS: Justin Gordon (tenor saxophone), Bill Perkins (baritone saxophone), Don Lodice (tenor saxophone), Don Raffell (tenor saxophone), Abe Most (clarinet)

V.I.P.'S BOOGIE
LEADER: Glen Gray TRUMPETS: Pete Candoli, Conrad Gozzo, Uan Rasey, Manny Klein, Shorty Sherock TROMBONES: Milt Bernhart, Joe Howard, Ed Kusby, George Roberts SAXOPHONES: Gus Bivona, Chuck Gentry, Skeets Herfurt, Julie Jacob, Babe Russin PIANO: Ray Sherman GUITAR: Jack Marshall BASS: Mike Rubin DRUMS: Nick Fatool SOLOS: Chuck Gentry (baritone saxophone), Gus Bivona (clarinet)

ACROSS THE ALLEY FROM THE ALAMO
LEADER: Billy May TRUMPETS: Pete Candoli, John Audino, Ray Triscari, Uan Rasey, Chuck Findley TROMBONES: Joe Howard, Dick Nash, Lew McCreary, Lloyd Ulyate, Phil Teele SAXOPHONES: Les Robinson, Abe Most, Justin Gordon, Don Lodice, Bill Perkins PIANO: Ray Sherman GUITAR: Jack Marshall BASS: Rolly Bundock DRUMS: Nick Fatool SOLO: Don Lodice (tenor saxophone) VOCAL: Eileen Wilson

BINGO, BANGO, BOFFO
LEADER: Billy May TRUMPETS: John Audino, Ray Triscari, Shorty Sherock, Uan Rasey, John Best TROMBONES: Joe Howard, Dick Nash, Lew McCreary, Ed Kusby SAXOPHONES: Les Robinson, Willie Schwartz, Don Lodice, Justin Gordon, Chuck Gentry PIANO: Ray Sherman GUITAR: Jack Marshall BASS: Rolly Bundock DRUMS: Nick Fatool SOLOS: Pete Candoli (trumpet), Lloyd Ulyate (trombone), Don Lodice (tenor saxophone)

LEAN BABY
Same as ALL OF ME. SOLOS: Don Raffell (tenor saxophone), Ray Sherman (piano)

HOT TODDY
LEADER: Billy May TRUMPETS: John Audino, John Best, Ray Triscari, Uan Rasey TROMBONES: Joe Howard, Lew McCreary, Ed Kusby SAXOPHONES: Les Robinson, Willie Schwartz, Don Lodice, Justin Gordon, Chuck Gentry PIANO: Ray Sherman GUITAR: Jack Marshall BASS: Rolly Bundock DRUMS: Nick Fatool

THE DOODLETOWN FIFERS
LEADER: Billy May TRUMPETS: John Best, Uan Rasey, Shorty Sherock TROMBONES: Joe Howard, Dick Nash, Lew McCreary SAXOPHONES: Willie Schwartz, Abe Most, Justin Gordon, Bill Perkins PIANO: Ray Sherman GUITAR: Jack Marshall BASS: Rolly Bundock DRUMS: Nick Fatool PERCUSSION: Larry Bunker, Gene Estes HARP: Verlye Brilhart TUBA: John Bambridge ELECTRIC GUITAR: Bob Bain

CUTE
Same as THE KID FROM RED BANK. SOLOS: Justin Gordon (flute), Nick Fatool (drums)

INTERLUDE
LEADER: Billy May TROMBONES: Joe Howard, Dick Nash, Lew McCreary, Lloyd Ulyate, Phil Teele PIANO: Ray Sherman GUITAR: Jack Marshall BASS: Rolly Bundock DRUMS: Nick Fatool SOLO: Ray Sherman (piano)

PUSSY WILLOW
LEADER: Billy May TRUMPETS: John Audino, Shorty Sherock, Pete Candoli, Ray Triscari, Uan Rasey TROMBONES: Joe Howard, Dick Nash, Lloyd Ulyate, Lew McCreary SAXOPHONES: Les Robinson, Willie Schwartz, Don Lodice, Justin Gordon, Chuck Gentry PIANO: Ray Sherman GUITAR: Jack Marshall BASS: Rolly Bundock DRUMS: Nick Fatool SOLO: Justin Gordon (tenor saxophone)

ARTISTRY JUMPS
LEADER: Billy May TRUMPETS: Pete Candoli, Ray Triscari, John Audino, Uan Rasey, Bud Brisbois, TROMBONES: Joe Howard, Dick Nash, Lew McCreary, Lloyd Ulyate, Phil Teele SAXOPHONES: Les Robinson, Abe Most, Justin Gordon, Don Lodice, Bill Perkins PIANO: Ray Sherman GUITAR: Jack Marshall BASS: Rolly Bundock DRUMS: Nick Fatool SOLOS: Justin Gordon (tenor saxophone), Ray Sherman (piano)

NIGHT TRAIN
LEADER: Glen Gray TRUMPETS: Conrad Gozzo, Manny Klein, Joe Graves, Shorty Sherock, Uan Rasey TROMBONES: Joe Howard, Lew McCreary, Si Zentner, Milt Bernhart SAXOPHONES: Abe Most, Skeets Herfurt, Plas Johnson, Chuck Gentry, Babe Russin PIANO: Ray Sherman GUITAR: Jack Marshall BASS: Mike Rubin DRUMS: Irv Cottler SOLO: Milt Bernhart (trombone)

KEEN AND PEACHY
LEADER: Billy May TRUMPETS: John Best, Uan Rasey, Shorty Sherock, John Audino, Bud Brisbois TROMBONES: Dick Nash, Joe Howard, Lloyd Ulyate SAXOPHONES: Les Robinson, Justin Gordon, Don Lodice, Don Raffell, Bill Perkins PIANO: Ray Sherman GUITAR: Jack Marshall BASS: Rolly Bundock DRUMS: Nick Fatool SOLOS: Don Raffell (tenor saxophone), Justin Gordon (tenor saxophone), Lew McCreary (trombone), Bill Perkins (baritone saxophone), Pete Candoli (trumpet), Bud Brisbois (high trumpet)

STAR BURST
Same as V.I.P.'s BOOGIE. SOLOS: Nick Fatool (drums), Conrad Gozzo (trumpet), Pete Candoli (trumpet)

BENJIE'S BUBBLE
LEADER: Billy May TRUMPETS: Pete Candoli, Shorty Sherock, John Audino, Uan Rasey TROMBONES: Dick Nash, Joe Howard, Lew McCreary SAXOPHONES: Les Robinson, Willie Schwartz, Julie Jacob, Justin Gordon, Bill Perkins PIANO: Ray Sherman GUITAR: Jack Marshall BASS: Rolly Bundock DRUMS: Nick Fatool SOLOS: Abe Most (clarinet), Ray Sherman (piano)

ORCHESTRA MANAGER: Abe Siegel
MIXER: Rex Updegraft

Discography

The original recordings of the
selections re-created in this volume

THE KID FROM RED BANK
*Composer and arranger: Neal Hefti. Recorded
for Roulette October 21, 1957*
TRUMPETS: Wendell Culley, Snooky Young,
Thad Jones, Joe Newman, Harold Baker *or*
Quincy Jones TROMBONES: Henry Coker, Al
Grey, Benny Powell SAXOPHONES: °Marshal
Royal, Eddie Davis, Frank Wess, Frank Foster,
Charlie Fowlkes PIANO: Count Basie GUITAR:
Freddie Green BASS: Eddie Jones DRUMS:
Sonny Payne

SATIN DOLL
*Composer and arranger: Duke Ellington. Re-
corded for Capitol April 6, 1953*
TRUMPETS: Ray Nance, Clark Terry, Willie
Cook, Cat Anderson TROMBONES: Quentin Jack-
son, Juan Tizol, Britt Woodman SAXOPHONES:
Russell Procope, Jimmy Hamilton, Rick Hender-
son, Paul Gonsalves, Harry Carney PIANO:
Duke Ellington BASS: Wendell Marshall DRUMS:
George Ballard

SWANEE RIVER BOOGIE
*Composer: Stephen Foster. Arranger: Tutti
Camarata. Recorded for Decca February 27,
1953*
TRUMPETS: Chris Griffin, Billy Butterfield, Yank
Lawson TROMBONES: Lou McGarity, Jack Sat-
terfield, Frank Saracco, Phil Giardina SAXO-
PHONES: Hymie Shertzer, Al Klink PIANO:
Bernie Leighton GUITAR: Carmen Mastren
BASS: Eddie Safranski DRUMS: Don Lamond

JUST A-SITTIN' AND A-ROCKIN'
*Composers: Duke Ellington and Billy Strayhorn.
Lyricist: Lee Gaines. Arranger: Gene Roland.
Recorded for Capitol October 30, 1945*
TRUMPETS: Buddy Childers, Ray Wetzel, John
Anderson, Russ Burgher, Bob Lymperis TROM-
BONES: Fred Zito, Jimmy Simms, Milt Kabak,
Bart Varsalona SAXOPHONES: Al Anthony, Boots
Mussulli, Vido Musso, Bob Cooper, Bob Gioga
PIANO: Stan Kenton GUITAR: Bob Ahern BASS:
Eddie Safranski DRUMS: Ralph Collier VOCAL:
June Christy

ALL OF ME
*Composer: Gerald Marks. Arranger: °Billy May.
Recorded for Capitol June 25, 1951*
TRUMPETS: °Conrad Gozzo, °Manny Klein,
°Uan Rasey, °John Best TROMBONES: °Si
Zentner, °Tommy Pederson, Murray McEachern,
°Ed Kusby SAXOPHONES: °Skeets Herfurt,
°Willie Schwartz, Ted Nash, Fred Falensby,
°Chuck Gentry PIANO: Buddy Cole GUITAR:
°Al Hendrickson BASS: Joe Mondragon DRUMS:
Alvin Stoller

APRIL IN PARIS
*Composer: Vernon Duke. Arranger: William
Davis. Recorded for Clef July 26, 1955*
TRUMPETS: Wendell Culley, Reunald Jones,
Thad Jones, Joe Newman TROMBONES: Henry
Coker, Bill Hughes, Benny Powell SAXOPHONES:
°Marshal Royal, Bill Graham, Frank Wess,
Frank Foster, Charlie Fowlkes PIANO: Count
Basie GUITAR: Freddie Green BASS: Eddie
Jones DRUMS: Sonny Payne

THE CONTINENTAL
*Composer: Con Conrad. Arranger: Bill Finegan.
Recorded for Victor March 11, 1949*
TRUMPETS: Vernon Arslan, Jack Dougherty,
Chris Griffin, Chuck Peterson, Charlie Shavers
TROMBONES: Tommy Dorsey, Nick Di Maio,
Buddy Morrow, °Dick Noel SAXOPHONES: Billy
Ainsworth, Sid Cooper, Babe Fresk, Boomie
Richman, Marty Berman PIANO: Paul Smith
GUITAR: Barry Galbraith BASS: Norman Seelig
DRUMS: Louis Bellson

EARLY AUTUMN
*Composers: Ralph Burns and Woody Herman.
Arranger: Ralph Burns. Recorded for Capitol
December 30, 1948*
TRUMPETS: Ernie Royal, Bernie Glow, Stan
Fishelson, Red Rodney, Shorty Rogers TROM-
BONES: Earl Swope, Bill Harris, Ollie Wilson,
Bob Swift CLARINET: Woody Herman SAXO-
PHONES: Sam Marowitz, Al Cohn, Zoot Sims,
Stan Getz, Serge Chaloff PIANO: Lou Levy
BASS: Chubby Jackson DRUMS: Don Lamond
VIBRAPHONE: Terry Gibbs

THE CHAMP
*Composer: Dizzy Gillespie. Arranger: Reg
Owen. Recorded for London Decca April 27,
1953.*
TRUMPETS: Duncan Campbell, Bobby Pratt,
Stan Reynolds, Ronnie Hughes TROMBONES:
Don Lusher, Jimmy Coombes, Wally Smith,
Ric Kennedy SAXOPHONES: Danny Moss, Henry
McKenzie, Roy Wilcox, Les Gilbert, George
Hunter PIANO: Frank Horrox GUITAR: Ernie
Shear BASS: Johnny Hawksworth DRUMS:
Ronnie Verrell

SO RARE
*Composer: Jerry Herst. Lyricist: Jack Sharpe.
Arranger: Lew Douglas. Recorded for Fraternity
Records November 11, 1956*
ALTO SAXOPHONE: Jimmy Dorsey TROMBONE
AND RHYTHM SECTIONS: Unknown VOCAL:
Artie Malvin Singers

ST. LOUIS BLUES MARCH
*Composer: William C. Handy. Arranger: Jerry
Gray. Recorded July-December 1943 as a
V-Disc, released by Victor 1955*
TRUMPETS: Zeke Zarchy, Stephen Steck, Walter
Holland, Jack Steele, Bernie Privin TROM-
BONES: Jimmy Priddy, Larry Hall, Jim Harwood,
Dick Halliburton SAXOPHONES: Hank Freeman,
Vincent Carbone, Jack Ferrier, Peanuts Hucko
PIANO: Louis Stein GUITAR: Carmen Mastren
BASS: Trigger Alpert DRUMS: Ray McKinley

THE PEANUT VENDOR
*Composer: Moises Simons. Arranger: Stan Ken-
ton. Recorded for Capitol December 6, 1947*
TRUMPETS: Buddy Childers, Ray Wetzel, Chico
Alvarez, Ken Hanna, Al Porcino TROMBONES:
°Milt Bernhart, Harry Forbes, Harry Betts,
Eddie Bert, Bart Varsalona SAXOPHONES:
George Weidler, Art Pepper, Bob Cooper,
Warner Weidler, Bob Gioga PIANO: Stan Ken-
ton GUITAR: Laurindo Almeida BASS: Eddie
Safranski DRUMS: Shelly Manne PERCUSSION:
Jack Costanzo (bongos), Frank "Machito"
Grillo (maracas), Carlos Vidal (conga), Jose
Luis Mangual (timbales)

LI'L DARLIN'
*Composer and arranger: Neal Hefti. Recorded
for Roulette May 26, 1958*
TRUMPETS: Thad Jones, Snooky Young, Wen-
dell Culley, Joe Newman TROMBONES: Henry
Coker, Al Grey, Benny Powell SAXOPHONES:
°Marshal Royal, Frank Wess, Billy Mitchell,
Frank Foster, Charlie Fowlkes PIANO: Count
Basie GUITAR: Freddie Green BASS: Eddie
Jones DRUMS: Sonny Payne

TANGO BLUES
*Composer and arranger: Harry James. Recorded
for Columbia April 11, 1951*
TRUMPETS: Harry James, Nick Buono, Everett
McDonald, Phil Cook, Ralph Osborn TROM-
BONES: Ziggy Elmer, Tommy Greco, Jimmy
Palmer, °Lew McCreary SAXOPHONES: Frank
Polifroni, James Cook, Jack Ordean, Mascagni
Ruffo, Bob Poland PIANO: Bruce McDonald
GUITAR: Bob Bain BASS: Ed Mihelich DRUMS:
Alvin Stoller

CARAVAN
*Composers: Duke Ellington and Juan Tizol.
Arranger: David Carroll. Recorded for Mercury
in 1953*
TRUMPET: Corny Panico TROMBONE: Paul
Crumbaugh SAXOPHONE: Jack Gaylo PIANO:
Matt Alagna GUITARS: Earl Backus, Remo
Biondi DRUMS: Henry Riggs (Other musicians
unknown)

FOUR BROTHERS
*Composer and arranger: Jimmy Guiffre. Re-
corded for Columbia December 27, 1947*
TRUMPETS: Ernie Royal, Bernie Glow, Stan
Fishelson, Shorty Rogers, Markie Markowitz
TROMBONES: Earl Swope, Ollie Wilson, Bob
Swift CLARINET: Woody Herman SAXOPHONES:
Sam Marowitz, Herbie Steward, Stan Getz,
Zoot Sims, Serge Chaloff PIANO: Fred Otis
GUITAR: Gene Sargent BASS: Walt Yoder
DRUMS: Don Lamond

V.I.P.'S BOOGIE
*Composer and arranger: Duke Ellington. Re-
corded for Columbia May 10, 1951*
TRUMPETS: Harold Baker, Fats Ford, Cat
Anderson, Nelson Williams, Ray Nance TROM-
BONES: Quentin Jackson, Britt Woodman, Juan
Tizol CLARINET: Jimmy Hamilton SAXOPHONES:
Jimmy Hamilton, Russell Procope, Willie Smith,
Paul Gonsalves, Harry Carney PIANO: Duke
Ellington BASS: Wendell Marshall DRUMS: Louis
Bellson

ACROSS THE ALLEY FROM THE ALAMO
*Composer and lyricist: Joe Greene. Arranger:
Pete Rugolo. Recorded for Capitol February
28, 1947*
TRUMPETS: Buddy Childers, Ray Wetzel, Chico
Alvarez, John Anderson, Ken Hanna TROM-
BONES: Kai Winding, Skip Layton, °Milt Bern-
hart, Harry Forbes, Bart Varsalona SAXO-
PHONES: Boots Mussulli, Eddie Meyers, Vido
Musso, Bob Cooper, Bob Gioga PIANO: Stan
Kenton GUITAR: Bob Ahern BASS: Eddie
Safranski DRUMS: Shelly Manne VOCAL: June
Christy

BINGO, BANGO, BOFFO
Composer and arranger: Bill Finegan. Recorded for Victor April 8, 1946
TRUMPETS: Vito Mangano, George Seaberg, Jack Dougherty, Ziggy Elman, Charlie Shavers TROMBONES: Tommy Dorsey, William Siegel, Tex Satterwhite, Greg Phillips SAXOPHONES: Sid Cooper, Buddy De Franco, Bruce Branson, Babe Fresk, Don Lodice PIANO: John Potoker GUITAR: Sam Herman BASS: Sid Block DRUMS: Alvin Stoller

LEAN BABY
Composer and arranger: °Billy May. Recorded for Capitol August 22, 1951
Same as ALL OF ME

HOT TODDY
Composer and arranger: Ralph Flanagan. Recorded for Victor June 5, 1957
TRUMPETS: Jimmy Maxwell, Bernie Glow, Rusty Dedrick TROMBONES: Bob Alexander, Phil Giacobbe, Billy Rauch, Warren Covington SAXOPHONES: Wolffe Taninbaum, Abraham Richmond, Stanley Webb, Walter Levinsky, Pete Fusco PIANO: Ralph Flanagan GUITAR: Danny Perri BASS: Milton Hinton DRUMS: Terry Snyder

THE DOODLETOWN FIFERS
Composers: Bill Finegan, Eddie Sauter and Henry Work. Arrangers: Bill Finegan and Eddie Sauter. Recorded for Victor May 12, 1952
TRUMPETS: Nick Travis, Bob Nichols, Joe Ferante TROMBONES: Willard Harris, Vernon Friley, Bart Varsalona SAXOPHONES: Sid Cooper, Babe Fresk, Al Klink, Boomie Richman,

Sol Schlinger PIANO: Ralph Burns GUITAR: Barry Galbraith BASS: Trigger Alpert DRUMS: Don Lamond, Walter Rosenberger HARP: °Verlye Brilhart TUBA: John Barber

INTERLUDE
Composer and arranger: Pete Rugolo. Recorded for Capitol December 22, 1947
TROMBONES: °Milt Bernhart, Harry Forbes, Harry Betts, Eddie Bert, Bart Varsalona PIANO: Stan Kenton GUITAR: Laurindo Almeida BASS: Eddie Safranski DRUMS: Shelly Manne

CUTE
Composer and arranger: Neal Hefti. Recorded for Roulette April 3, 1958
Same as LI'L DARLIN'. Flute solo: Frank Wess

PUSSY WILLOW
Composer and arranger: Bill Finegan. Recorded for Victor March 16, 1949
Same as THE CONTINENTAL except Chris Griffin and Buddy Morrow out, and Allen Hanlon (guitar) replaces Barry Galbraith

ARTISTRY JUMPS
Composer and arranger: Stan Kenton. Recorded for Capitol October 30, 1945
Same as JUST A-SITTIN' AND A-ROCKIN' without vocal

NIGHT TRAIN
Composer: Jimmy Forrest. Arranger: Dick Rhodes. Recorded for Victor April 12, 1952
TRUMPETS: A. Russetti, C. Blaisdell, Sam Scavone TROMBONES: F. Angst, Bob Alexander,

P. Gilmore SAXOPHONES: Hal Miles, S. Goldfarb, Patrick Balbo, H. Wuest PIANO: Bill Jacob BASS: Dick Nivison DRUMS: °Irv Cottler

KEEN AND PEACHY
Composers and arrangers: Ralph Burns and Shorty Rogers. Recorded for Columbia December 24, 1947
Same as FOUR BROTHERS

STAR BURST
Composers: Eddie Finckel and Gene Krupa. Arranger: Dick Taylor. Recorded for Columbia February 5, 1947
TRUMPETS: Armand Anelli, °Ray Triscari, Don Fagerquist, Al Porcino TROMBONES: Dick Taylor, Jack Zimmerman, Emil Mazanec, Clay Harvey SAXOPHONES: Sam Marowitz, Jack Schwartz, Charlie Kennedy, Buddy Wise, Mitch Melnick PIANO: Tommy Eanelli GUITAR: Bob Lesher BASS: Bob Strahl DRUMS: Gene Krupa

BENJIE'S BUBBLE
Composers: Benny Goodman and Joe Bushkin. Arranger: Joe Bushkin. Recorded for Columbia August 29, 1946
TRUMPETS: °John Best, Nate Kazebier, Dick Mains, Mickey McMickle TROMBONES: Cutty Cutshall, Leon Cox FRENCH HORN: Addison Collins CLARINET: Benny Goodman SAXOPHONES: Hymie Shertzer, Larry Molinelli, Cliff Strickland, Lester Clarke, Al Klink PIANO: Joe Bushkin GUITAR: Mike Bryan BASS: Barney Spieler DRUMS: Louis Bellson

---

°Took part in one or more of the re-creations in this volume

ACKNOWLEDGMENTS

A number of musicians, bandleaders, arrangers, singers, managers, songwriters and others knowledgable on swing music and other subjects helped with source material for this book. The editors of TIME-LIFE RECORDS wish to thank particularly the following for their assistance: Walter C. Allen, Margaret Ashford, Earl Backus, Louis Bellson, Milt Bernhart, Ray Biondi, Billy Butterfield, Joe Bushkin, Ralph Burns, Tutti Camarata, Harry Carney, David Carroll, Pete Clarke, Cozy Cole, Eddie Condon, Warren Covington, Helen Oakley Dance, Stanley Dance, Sam Donahue, Frank Driggs, Jack Egan, Roy Eldridge, Duke Ellington, Mercer Ellington, Don Fagerquist, Eddie Finckel, Bill Finegan, Ralph Flanagan, Bud Freeman, Milt Gabler, Joe Garland, Dizzy Gillespie, Justin Gordon, Eddie Grady, Joe Greene, Jimmy Guiffre, Thornton Hagert, Lionel Hampton, Martin Haniffy, Jack Hartley, Neal Hefti, Joe Helbock, Budd Johnson, Gene Krupa, Mary Louise Lanci, Norman Lester, Lawrence Lucie, Shelly Manne, Gerald Marks, Herbert Marks, Ralph Marterie, Billy May, Ray McKinley, Jimmy McLin, Johnny Mercer, Buddy Morrow, Vido Musso, Sam Nastico, Albert Nicholas, Anita O'Day, Larry Parker, Beverly Peer, Specs Powell, Russell Procope, Les Robinson, Pete Rugolo, Eddie Safranski, Edgar Sampson, Vic Schoen, Dean Shaffner, Charlie Shavers, Ray Sherman, Shorty Sherock, Hymie Shertzer, Maxine Sullivan, Dave Usher, Miriam van Aernam, Bart Varsalona, Sarah Vaughan, Earl Warren, Sandy Williams.

Time Inc. departments and staff members who were helpful: Anne Drayton and Carmela Lotrecchiano of the offices of LIFE's Director of Photography; Anne Angus, Jim Bready, Champ Clark, Bob Delaney, Kent Demaret, Nancy Faber, Marcia Gauger, Robert Parker and Barbara Wilkins of the Time-Life News Service; Doris O'Neil, Chief, Picture Collection; George Karas and Herbert Orth of the Photographic Laboratory.